A CELEBRATION OF SALMON RIVERS

a celebration of

SALMON RIVERS

©NASF and R. Randolph Ashton, 2007

Graphic design: Lars Gundersen

Photo editing: R. Randolph Ashton and Lars Gundersen

Edited by John B. Ashton and Adrian Latimer

Graphic production: Jepsen&Co, Copenhagen, Denmark tlf +45 3332 5363

Printed by Nørhaven Book, Viborg DK

Printed in Denmark 2007

ISBN 978-0-8117-0279-9: Stackpole Books, USA

All photographs by R. Randolph Ashton

except for the following:

page 6: Clarence House, page 9: Terry Ring, page 14: Michel Roggo,

page 22-25: Dale Spartas, page 76: Vivvi Orrason, page 162 middle: Matt Harris,

page 169: Tarquin Millington-Drake, page 228 & 233: Palle Uhd Jepsen,

page 230 top: Martin Gloor, page 230 bottom: Daniel Luther, page 232: Martin Neptune

A CELEBRATION OF
SALMON RIVERS

photography by R. Randolph Ashton

To: Randy

Hope you enjoy the book!

Rob Ashton

STACKPOLE
BOOKS

Everyone who fishes for salmon will have a favourite river. The affection may have grown from days of success, from days of great challenge or simply from days spent in particularly wonderful surroundings. The reasons for our choices make good reading, complete with tales of triumph and disaster, on those many days when we can't be on a river. So I welcome Orri Vigfússon's initiative in asking so many expert anglers to extol the virtues of their own favourite rivers.

I have been fortunate enough to fish quite a few salmon rivers over the last half century or so, and I started fishing on the River Dee at about the age of seven. My beloved Grandmother's affection for the Dee was infectious and I am profoundly grateful for the time she spent gently encouraging my passion for salmon, not just as a sporting quarry but also as a vital indicator of the health of wild rivers throughout the North Atlantic. I still fish the Dee on a few occasions every year, and we are beginning to see some signs of recovery, though there is still a long way to go before we return to the days when a single day's leave from the Royal Navy, on the opening day of the season, produced five large, fresh Spring fish! But perhaps my most special memories are reserved for the Hofsa river in Iceland...

At a time when new books about salmon proliferate, it is heartening to see a book that puts the emphasis on the rivers, rather than the fish. We all know, and none better than Orri Vigfússon, that many of the salmon's problems lie at sea, or in the estuaries. Yet sensitive habitat restoration, expensive and labour-intensive though it is, also has an important part to play in rebuilding stocks.

I hope this most evocative of books will encourage even more fishermen to support the work of the North Atlantic Salmon Fund. Together with other organizations, such as the Atlantic Salmon Trust and the Salmon and Trout Association, the Fund has made huge progress towards its goal of ending interceptory netting, with proper compensation for the netsmen. I have watched the work of the Fund with interest and admiration for the last fifteen years and wish them every continued success.

It isn't impossible to think of a time when runs of salmon into all the rivers described in this book go from strength to strength. In addition to ending interceptory netting and improving river habitats, we would need to improve salmon farming techniques to protect wild salmon and sea trout from its ill effects. The final measure is entirely in our own hands. The prize of restoring and maintaining our great Atlantic salmon heritage is surely worth the effort.

DEDICATION

Photo taken by Terry Ring on the Laxá in Kjós July, 1999

The North Atlantic Salmon Fund dedicates this *A Celebration of Salmon Rivers* to John Hadley Nicanor Hemingway, one of the world's greatest fly fishermen and conservationists. Jack was a member of the Board of Directors of NASF before his untimely death in 2000. Jack fished many of the rivers depicted in this book. He would have loved to have fished them all.

The following, an excerpt from Tom McGuane's wonderful *"The Longest Silence; A Life in Fishing"*, captures the true essence of this wonderful man:

> "Jack Hemingway joined us for a day. He was going from river to river and would continue to do so, he said, until every source of funds had dried up. Few people who were parachuted behind German lines in World War II would've thought to bring a fly rod, but Jack did. To this superficial observer he seemed a happy man. In any case, something contributed to giving a seventy-five year old the enthusiasm and energy of a boy. I kept thinking of Jack as "Bumby," the infant of his father's *Moveable Feast,* baby-sat by F. Puss, the cat, and imagining the tempestuous times in which he'd grown up in France among the century's most evolved characters. Jack turned out great, and a real fisherman. He called his most recent birthday party The Son Also Rises. It was a pleasure to sit near one splendid river and talk about others with someone who had lived so fully for such a long time."

Below Forks Pool, Grand Cascapedia

TABLE OF CONTENTS

Low water under Kildonan Bridge, Helmsdale

Orri Vigfússon on the Selá

INTRODUCTION

Our Atlantic salmon rivers, represented by the magnificent examples depicted in this book, are the primary reasons we strive to protect the wild Atlantic salmon. A salmon river devoid of wild fish is a tragedy for mankind. A river once again teaming with wild fish is the dream that motivates us.

Fifteen years ago the North Atlantic Salmon Fund (NASF) was launched as a last-ditch effort to prevent what then seemed to be the likely extinction of the wild Atlantic salmon. Over the past 15 years the commercial netting of Atlantic salmon on the high seas, which had decimated Atlantic salmon stocks, has been virtually eliminated and many of the nets within territorial waters have been bought out.

A great victory for the Atlantic salmon and mankind was recently won when, in a complete reversal of its previous policies, the Irish government decided that its driftnet fishery must end. These nets, operating off the west and south coasts of Ireland, had been killing wild salmon by the hundreds of thousands every year. They were not only seriously depleting salmon stocks in Irish rivers, they also intercepted many salmon that would otherwise have returned to struggling rivers in the UK and continental Europe. NASF, with help from other like-minded organizations and governments, worked ceaselessly over many years to eliminate these driftnets, recognizing that programs to restore salmon populations were largely futile as long as these nets were operating. Now the work of restoring abundant salmon runs in Ireland and other European countries holds renewed promise.

It will take time. Many of the rivers in question are so depleted that restoring a highly sustainable run of salmon will take years of concerted effort. But rivers in other parts of the North Atlantic are already beginning to see the benefits of our efforts over the past 15 years. There are reports of a distinct and in some cases substantial upturn in runs of multi-sea-winter (MSW) salmon on both sides of the Atlantic. These large fish are much the most valuable salmon to run our rivers, both in terms of their sporting value and their capacity to produce large numbers of healthy eggs that are usually more viable than those produced by grilse.

It is still too early to claim that the wild salmon's future is assured. But there are encouraging signs that the corner that leads to the recovery of Atlantic salmon stocks may have been turned. NASF is publishing this book to celebrate our wonderful Atlantic salmon rivers and to inspire us all to continue our efforts to make the dream of rivers once again teaming with salmon a reality.

Orri Vigfússon, Founder and Chairman of NASF

It is, of course, the waters off Greenland that produce MSW salmon and it was here that the first great slaughter took place once the locations of the salmon's sea feeding grounds were discovered. The destruction wrought by an international fishing free-for-all was so great that it quickly led to a slump in the stocks of Canada's formerly prolific salmon rivers. It brought about the near demise of the wild Atlantic salmon in the rivers of the USA, already depleted by centuries of habitat abuse.

It also led to the launch of NASF when we recognized the dangers and decided to act. The feeding grounds off Greenland and the Faroe Islands were at risk of being completely denuded of feeding salmon. I went to Greenland and the Faroes, met with the fishermen and negotiated agreements with them whereby they would curtail commercial fishing for salmon in exchange for compensation and our commitment to help them develop alternate ways of earning a living. Today, apart from a small fishery in Greenland that catches a few salmon for limited domestic consumption, the moratorium on killing salmon by Greenland and Faroe fishermen continues. Thanks to the lucrative alternative fisheries for snow crab and lumpfish caviar that NASF has encouraged and financial assistance from NASF's loyal supporters and other organizations, notably the Atlantic Salmon Federation in respect of Greenland, we expect to be able to continue to protect the sea feeding grounds indefinitely.

NASF has become a very successful international private sector organization, recognized by every government that has interests in the future of the Atlantic salmon and given charitable status in some countries. NASF adopted the most obvious way to cure the salmon's ills. It has increased the numbers of salmon that survive to spawn by saving them from the fishmonger's slab. It has been estimated that NASF has now rescued between ten and twenty million salmon from commercial fishing and given these fish the opportunity to return to their native rivers to spawn.

This could have been a very unpopular medicine. But the cure was made palatable by paying commercial fishermen to volunteer to stop salmon fishing and by identifying other forms of work for them. This requires NASF to raise substantial funds each year, but it is the one remedy that works and the price we pay to save the lives of wild salmon is a fantastic bargain considering the benefits.

NASF also recognizes that much of the money to pay for this must come from the angling community. Their donations would not be forthcoming if the rod

fishermen, who take only a small percentage of the stock, were prevented from fishing. In return, anglers no longer take home all the salmon they catch. Most rivers have strict restrictions that prevent their rods from killing more than a few salmon annually and NASF has persuaded many sport fishermen to release all or most of the salmon they catch.

Having won the backing of a number of other organizations concerned with the survival and restoration of wild salmon stocks, NASF vigorously lobbies governments, politicians and other influential individuals. We are determined to end damaging management practices and advance environmental standards.

NASF has introduced a new vision of abundant wild salmon stocks so that future generations will know and appreciate the beauty and strength of the wild Atlantic salmon. It believes that the fruits of this recovery should be enjoyed by every nation whose rivers or seas produce, feed or form migratory routes for wild salmon. Most of the rivers depicted in this book have benefited and will continue to benefit from our activities.

We all must recognize, however, that *Salmo salar* is still under threat in and around the rivers of much of its North Atlantic range. We must be prepared to make the protection and conservation of the resource an absolute priority. Each year NASF must raise substantial sums to fund the various agreements that protect the salmon from commercial exploitation. And a number of locally destructive commercial fisheries still remain, which will undoubtedly require new agreements and additional funding. We need your help.

The funds this book will raise will help add new impetus to our task. That is why, on behalf of NASF, I would like to thank all those who have so generously contributed to its content and its production. Our thanks also go to you, dear reader, for adding it to your library.

Orri Vigfússon

CANADA

LABRADOR

Eagle

QUEBEC

Moise

NEWFOUNDLAND

Gulf of
St Lawrence

*Grand
Cascapedia*

Bonaventure

Restigouche

Miramichi

Quebec

NEW
BRUNSWICK

NOVA SCOTIA

Peter and Parker Corbin above The Rapids, Moise

BONAVENTURE

Most anglers who have fished it affectionately refer to Quebec's Bonaventure River as "the Bonnie". Located in the Gaspé Peninsula, where legendary salmon rivers are numerous, it has long been one of the region's most cherished. Named after Saint Bonaventure, it attracted the attention of royalty as early as 1697, when the King of France initially began granting rights over the river. Called "Wagamet" (clear water) by the local MicMac natives, its headwaters originate in the *Parc de la Gaspésie* in the Chic Choc Mountains deep in the heart of the Gaspé. Eventually feeding into the *Baies des Chaleurs*, it runs for 123 km through 103 named pools. Currently supporting an average annual run of 2,000 salmon, it has a long history of private fishing lodges as well as providing angling opportunities to the general public. The Bonnie provides excellent wading. And when fished by canoe, with guide and anchorman, the experience is traditional Canadian Atlantic salmon fishing at its best.

Atlantic salmon fishermen learn to treasure different rivers for their uniqueness. The Bonnie is not a rough and tumble river like the Grand Cascapedia or the Moise. She is an elegant and restrained lady with almost unbelievably clear water tinged in emerald, a stone and pebble bottom mottled in grays and tans and a current swift and hard at the top of a run, then smooth as silk in the glide. These enticing qualities provide an added benefit to the angler - I have not fished any river more suitable for sight casting to salmon with a dry fly.

When you first arrive for your week on the Bonnie, you begin with great enthusiasm, but your senses, dulled by the urban environment where most of us are forced to earn our living, are not yet acclimated to the river's intricacies - the flow patterns, bottom structure and varying depths. You strain to see the fish that your guide spots so easily. He stands by your side pointing - "there... there... there... and there". After a while your senses re-attune. A light pastel indicates shallow water, a rich dark blue, deep pools. You begin to recognize the shadow, shape and slight tail movement that signify a resting salmon. Suddenly you notice five and then, incredibly, fifty.

To arrive on the Bonaventure on a crisp cool morning and watch as the sun gradually crosses the river to display one or two hundred salmon lined up throughout the pool, awaiting the conditions to move upstream, is truly exhilarating. Seeing your magnificent quarry as it slowly and rhythmically

Elbow Pool

fins to maintain its holding position is thrilling. But it is also intimidating. My guide Laurent insists that I must first catch a salmon using a conventional wet fly before he allows me to use a dry. I guess he figures that once a successful day has been assured by conventional fishing techniques, I have earned the right to try to entice a large visible fish with a dry fly.

Salmon Pool

Virtually all anglers on the Bonaventure now voluntarily practice catch-and-release, as the serious challenges faced by wild Atlantic salmon are now broadly understood. And Quebec fishing regulations dictate that once you have "caught" (defined as having a hand on the leader) two salmon, you must stop fishing for the day. (Note: - Atlantic salmon fishing regulations in Canada are complicated, strict, vigorously enforced and vary depending on the province and river.) Most anglers in Canada understand and willingly accept the fact that such measures are essential to preserving the wonderful experience of fishing for wild Atlantic salmon. If you happen to be so lucky as to catch your limit on the Bonnie, you can retire early to the lodge to reflect on your experience and share them with your other successful fishing partners. And an early return is a clear indication of your success to the less fortunate who arrive later!

Mark Brefka

Snake Pool

Home Pool, Rifflin' Hitch Lodge

EAGLE

Every river has to start somewhere, and Labrador's famed Eagle River is no exception. But for a great Atlantic salmon river, the Eagle's beginnings are rather humble. Its headwaters lie on the high plateau of the Mealy Mountains to the southwest of Goose Bay, a series of interconnecting tea-colored lakes and streams. These small streams join together to form the Eagle and then wander through wide steadies, white water rapids, deep gorges and a few steep waterfalls more than 200 km before reaching saltwater at Sandwich Bay.

The wilderness through which the river runs was originally explored by angling pioneer Lee Wulff, flying his small pontoon-equipped single-engine plane, "Yellow Bird". He found not only salmon, but also the unique Eastern Brook Trout which inhabit these waters. These beautiful trout average four to six pounds and often go much higher.

There is a fork in the Eagle about 100 km from the river mouth on Sandwich Bay. The majority of the salmon which enter the river from the Labrador Sea near the coastal community of Cartwright do not enter the southern branch. They choose the north branch which feeds from Park Lake and other interior watersheds and eventually lead them to the pure gravel and constant currents they seek as their spawning grounds.

The Eagle is widely known among anglers for its tremendous runs of salmon. The most popular area to fish, and clearly the most accessible, is near the river's mouth. For decades there have been outfitters operating there, offering superb angling from late June through mid-August when the major runs of salmon enter from the sea. Provincial regulations require non-residents to utilize the services of outfitters and guides to enjoy the Eagle's recreational fishery. Though far from civilization, these facilities offer comfortable accommodations, fine food and seasoned guides that make fishing the Eagle a wonderful wilderness experience.

In earlier days a vibrant commercial fishery harvested most of the river's larger salmon. The Eagle became known primarily as a grilse river. But regulations have restricted the food fishery in recent years and each year more and more MSW salmon return to the river. Specimens of 20 to 30 pounds, with an occasional even larger fish, are caught by sport fishers today.

Purgatory Pool

A new road system has opened up the Labrador coast to vehicles, but does not reach the Eagle River. Due to difficulty of access across the wide expanse of Sandwich Bay, most lodges are accessible only by float plane or helicopter flying out of Goose Bay. This limited access enables the Eagle to maintain its wilderness identity and its integrity as a world-class salmon river.

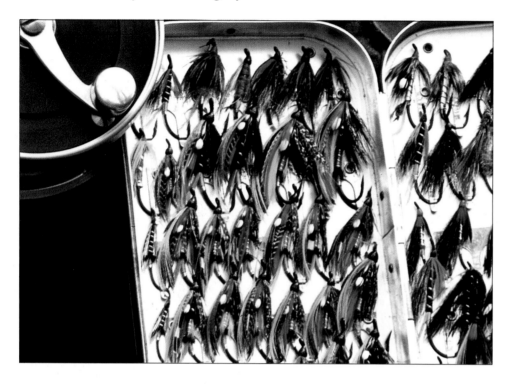

Most serious salmon fishermen have probably heard of the Eagle, whitch is in Labrador, and perhaps the Humber, which is in Newfoundland. But I doubt many are aware that some two-thirds of North America's recognized salmon rivers, nearly 200 in total, lie within the Province of Newfoundland and Labrador. The Province's long coastline, abundant supplies of clear, cool water, proximity to the winter feeding areas around Greenland and overall remoteness provide ideal habitat for the Atlantic salmon. Lesser known rivers such as the Exploits, Gander, Portland Creek, River of Ponds, Torrent, Terra Nova, Indian, Lomond and Garnish are all first rate salmon rivers that yield significant numbers of salmon to recreational fishermen annually. These rivers are also benefiting from provincial regulations which now limit commercial netting and the buy out of the Greenland nets orchestrated by NASF with the Atlantic Salmon Federation. I suggest you give the Eagle or one of these great other rivers a try – you will not be disappointed.

Len Rich

Playing Salmon in Purgatory Pool

GRAND CASCAPEDIA

THE SHORES OF EASTERN CANADA are blessed with scores of beautiful rivers, the summer retreats for tens of thousands of Atlantic salmon who find their sweet waters annually. Quebec's Gaspé Peninsula, bordered on its northern shore by the majestic St. Lawrence River that slips past the cities of Montreal and Quebec as it makes its way to the expanse of the Atlantic Ocean, is laced with many of the Dominion's more consistently productive rivers. The York, the beautiful St. John, the crystal clear waters of the Bonaventure, the Matapedia and the incomparable St. Anne are among the many fine Gaspé salmon rivers. But the signature river, the one that all anglers want to taste just once, is the Grand Cascapedia.

The source for the Grand Cascapedia is a series of lakes and small streams tucked in remote elevations of the Chic Choc Mountains that make their east to west traverse across the Gaspé. The branches join at the Forks to form pools with mythical names like Upper Lost Channel, Indian Crossing and, pacing the forty miles until it reaches places like Dun's Nest, Big Curley and the deep swirling, dark waters of Jack the Sailor, are over 150 named pools, most with over one hundred years of stories to tell, many of which still hold large pods of multi-sea-winter salmon, the sight of which can quicken the step of even the most jaundiced angler.

The first adventuresome anglers to visit the small estuary village of New Richmond arrived around 1850. The region was remote, and the few Acadians and Loyalists there shared the valley with a small band of natives, hunted and fished from the abundant shores of the Bay of Chaleur. In time a railroad serviced the southern coastline of the Gaspé, but the three sitting British governor-generals of Canada (Lord Lorne, Lord Lansdowne and Lord Stanley) who were given the exclusive fishing rights to the upper 40 miles of the Grand Cascapedia from 1879 to 1893, and who were to build camps on its shores, did not hear the sound of a train whistle during their tenure on the river. The few fishermen that did test some of the open riparian pools went home with tales of landing three salmon over 40 pounds in one day, or fish of over 50 pounds balanced on a camp scale.

The handful of wealthy men who took the lease on the waters formerly given to the governor-generals formed the exclusive Cascapedia Club. The members of the club, mostly wealthy American's with names like Frick, Vanderbilt, Phipps, and the leader of the pack, Robert G. Dun (Dun and Bradstreet),

Lower Lost Channel

self-regulated the pools that were theirs to fish, guarding their waters from the inexorable pressure of predators and publicity that many other Gaspé rivers were beginning to fall prey to. The salmon counts began to teeter after the Great Depression, but the average weight of the fish still clung to the 20 pound mark, and as nations recovered from WW II the river too held its own to the benefit of the small band of men and women who were lucky enough to test its waters.

Fortune has looked after this river. The deep, forested canyons that shoulder it have for over a century looked down on relatively few anglers, almost all of whom cared for the resource. Over the years the Grand Cascapedia has opened most portions of its carefully regulated waters to the public on a lottery basis so that people from all over the world can get their chance to be just yards from a salmon that might well be over 40 pounds. The river is unquestionably one of nature's great gifts, all in a setting that has changed little, with a run of large Atlantic salmon that is today unmatched in Canada. William Mershon, one of the early doyen's of the Grand Cascapedia, said it best: "It is a grand sport, and it is a grand river, and if one only will forget all about the size of the bag and give himself to the enjoyment of what nature has put before him, it is just about as near Heaven as can be."

Hoagy B. Carmichael

Indian Brook (above the Forks)

MIRAMICHI

Atlantic salmon rivers are some of the most beautiful places on earth and through my work with the Atlantic Salmon Federation ("ASF") it has been my good fortune to visit many of them. My favorite, not surprisingly, is the river I know best. It is the river I grew up fishing with my father and the one my wife and I now fish regularly with our daughters.

The Miramichi drains a huge watershed, flowing more than 800 km from its cold, clear wilderness headwater tributaries in central New Brunswick to its estuary and the Gulf of St. Lawrence. It is by far the most productive Atlantic salmon river in North America, if not the world. Most years anglers on the Miramichi catch as many salmon as on all other Canadian rivers combined. It has many fine tributaries, each with its own unique character and salmon runs. The larger ones, the Main Southwest, Northwest, Little Southwest, Sevogle, Cains, Renous and Dungarvon, are major salmon rivers in their own right.

The first runs of chrome bright salmon fresh from the sea begin entering the Miramichi in early June. These are extraordinary fish, perfect silver torpedoes that take the fly hard and fight with phenomenal strength and stamina. The runs continue more or less without interruption until October, my favorite time on the river. The days are cool, the water levels are more or less reliable, and the autumn scenery is spectacular. This is also the time of year when a large percentage of the fresh runs are comprised of repeat spawners, trophy salmon of 20, 30 and even 40 pounds and larger. Some of these monsters have survived the rigors of spawning as many as five times and to hook one is the thrill of a lifetime.

For the past 20 years my wife and I have shared a wonderful week together on the Miramichi in mid-October. Our now teenaged daughters joined us as soon as they were big enough to cast a fly. We have wonderful memories of great fish landed and even greater fish lost, and most importantly, time spent together surrounded by the wonders of nature and the beauty of this magnificent river.

While the Miramichi has always been a tremendously productive river, even it has suffered from the abuses of over-fishing and mismanagement in the past. Today, thankfully, it is rebounding, along with many other Canadian salmon rivers. Principle among the reasons for the recovery is the ASF's

Priceville Foot Bridge

31

successful campaign to convince the Canadian government to permanently buy out Canada's commercial salmon fishermen. More recently, ASF's collaboration with NASF to suspend Greenland's commercial salmon fishery has saved tens of thousands of large spawners bound for the Miramichi and other North American and European rivers. More fish and bigger fish are returning now that the maize of nets that once choked the salmon's ocean migration routes have been removed. Anglers have also contributed greatly to the salmon's recovery on the Miramichi by embracing catch-and-release and supporting local efforts to protect and restore habitat.

The tide is turning. As good as the angling has been on the Miramichi in recent years, many anglers, myself among them, believe the best days still lie ahead for this great river.

Bill Taylor

Dam Camp

Home Pool of Rocky Brook Camp

MOISE

THE MOISE IS A BIG, brawling river. From Lake Opocopa near the Labrador border it begins to cut its swathe of rapids, waterfalls and heavy runs through the Quebec wilderness before flowing into the St. Lawrence River not far from *Sept-Îles,* some 250 miles downriver. It is one of North America's three "big fish salmon rivers," and along with the Grand Cascapedia and the Restigouche, routinely produces salmon in excess of 30 pounds and occasionally 40. It is almost devoid of grilse. There are essentially two distinct runs – those in the 10 to 15 pound class and those which run from 18 to 23 pounds.

The Moise has two primary branches – the west branch, which is the main Moise, and the east branch, which is the Nipissis River. The two come together at the Forks approximately 28 miles from the St. Lawrence River. The salmon in the Nipissis tend to be long and lean. Those from the main branch are more stocky and torpedo-shaped. Both strains are extraordinarily strong. In fact, if there is one aspect of the Moise that dominates all others, it is the strength and stamina of its salmon. I know of no angler who has ever fished the Moise who does not conclude that the Moise salmon are the toughest and most determined salmon that they have ever caught.

Lee Wulff understood the importance of keeping the gene pool clean and pure in salmon rivers. This is the major reason why he was opposed to stocking salmon from one river into another. Like so many other things, Lee had this one right. I am no scientist, let alone a geneticist, but I believe the reason why the salmon of the Moise are so powerful is because the river itself is so rugged; it's heavy and deep with numerous rapids and waterfalls. It takes an athlete of superb strength, agility and stamina to traverse the Moise.

Another distinguishing feature of the Moise is that its main run of salmon tends to come through all at once, usually within a three-week period. When the run is on, the Moise Salmon Club water is the most productive salmon water that I have ever fished, and I have experienced times when it was impossible to cast a fly into the water without a rise, honestly! Another wonderful quality of Moise River salmon is their tendency to come back after an initial rise and refusal. As all salmon anglers will agree, there is nothing more exciting than a fish that rises repeatedly before eventually taking the fly. One time on the Moise I watched my brother Dave raise the same salmon 18 times. We knew it was the same fish because we could see it coming out of the dark, amber-colored water and over a light-colored rock before rising to the fly. Dave rose this fish on wets and dries of all sizes over a remarkable two-hour period.

The late Mitch Campbell, legendary manager of the Moise Salmon Club, estimated the annual salmon run on the Moise during the 1970's and 80's at 20,000 fish. For reasons not altogether understood, it is estimated that annual runs now average closer to 7000 fish – still quite respectable. As long as we continue to respect and preserve its wild and unique habitat and protect the Atlantic salmon as they feed in the North Atlantic and migrate to and from the river, the Moise should remain one of the world's finest salmon rivers.

Donal C. O'Brien, Jr.

Members Dining Room, Moise Club

Tail of Adams Pool

RESTIGOUCHE

Foot Bridge to Richard's Pool

FISHING FOR ATLANTIC SALMON is one of my favorite pastimes. I enjoy retreating into some of the most beautiful natural settings on this planet, the fellowship of good friends and testing my mettle against the finest of game fish. For a number of years I have had the good fortune to be invited to fish on the Restigouche, generally considered to be one of the finest salmon rivers in the world. No argument here!

Serge Desrosiers at Routhierville Bridge

The Restigouche is a wide, fast flowing river in a land of dense forests, log cabins nestled in birch groves, guides in rough woolen shirts and long canoes poled through fast rapids to large, deep pools. The name of the river is thought to have derived from the MicMac (or sometimes "Mi'kmaq") tribe's word meaning "five fingers", presumably reflecting the fact that five separate rivers, the Little Main Restigouche, Matapedia, Upsalquitch, Patapedia and Kedgwich, come together to form the main stem. This system drains a vast area of some 6,000 square miles of both New Brunswick and Quebec (the lower river is actually the boundary between these two provinces) and flows into the Gulf of St. Lawrence at the head of the Bay of Chaleur near the small village of Matapedia.

Page 38: Mocklers Island

In the mid 1800's fishing for salmon became in vogue in wealthy circles, and the Restigouche was accessible by boat from Boston, New York and Philadelphia. The fishermen who made this trip included the titans of industry at that time, with familiar names like Vanderbilt, Schyler, Lamont, Whitney and Tiffany. They built comfortable, often quite elegant, "cabins" along the banks, generally within a short walk to the best pools. The Ristigouche Salmon Club (originally spelled with an "i" as the second letter) was one of the first fishing clubs founded in North America (1880) and was regarded as the most exclusive, and wealthiest, club of that time.

No matter what you may think about the exclusivity that ruled for over a century on the Restigouche and still pertains to a large degree, it did have one very beneficial effect. The wealthy people who controlled the river, whether through self-interest or genuine respect for nature and conservation (I suspect a combination of both impulses), were good stewards of this great resource. Fishing was judiciously controlled, nets in the river mouth were bought out, stocking programs were implemented and development of the region was restrained. This, together with the remoteness of the river, meant that the Restigouche escaped many of the consequences of the Industrial Revolution and other human encroachments which have destroyed, or seriously impaired, so many other salmon rivers.

There is now public access to fishing on the Restigouche and the river is a favorite of canoeists. Fortunately, the Canadian Government now takes its responsibility over fishing waters seriously, and fresh water fishing, especially for salmon, is now tightly controlled. But government action alone will not be sufficient to protect our rivers and salmon, not to mention undoing the harm wrought by man's excesses over the years. This, I believe, is a responsibility we fishermen should eagerly assume. We are the primary beneficiaries of clean rivers and abundant runs of fish. There are few fishermen today with the financial resources of those whose "benign self-interest" helped maintain the fabulous fishing on the Restigouche, but there are certainly more of us now. What results we can achieve if we all do our part!

Paul Volcker

Pierre D'Amours fishing Richard's Pool

40

ICELAND

Laxá in Aðaldal

Selá

Hofsá

Vatnsdalsá

Viðidalsá

Norðurá

Langá

Þverá Kjarrá

Haffjarðará

Grímsá

Laxá in Leirársveit

Laxá in Kjós

● Reykjavík

Sheep above the Hofsá River

GRÍMSÁ

THE WATERFALL RUMBLES, birds sing and the morning sun reflects stunningly off the water's surface. It is like an indescribable dream to awaken on a beautiful summer morning in the Grímsá River fishing lodge, high above Laxfoss Falls. The view is of contrasting scenes which exemplify the variety of Icelandic fishing and evoke strong feelings for the beauty of an Icelandic fishing river. There before you are the vigorous falls of Laxfoss, the quiet flow of Stórlaxaflöt and, interwoven between black cliffs on both sides, the striking and impressive Svartistokkur.

The Grímsá River is one of the most famous and popular salmon rivers in Iceland, and also one of its prettiest. Its source is a lake near the ice cap-crowned Ok Mountain. It flows in a north-westerly direction through the narrow Lundarreykjardalur Valley to where it arrives at the larger Borgarfjördur Valley and empties into the glacial-fed Hvítá River from the southeast (the Norðurá and Þverá Kjarrá both enter the Hvítá on the opposite bank). It is a short hour's drive out of Reykjavík. Magnificent waterfalls and swift currents flowing over ledges are found in the downstream beats, where the salmon find good hiding places in the fissured rapids and runs. Further upstream the river winds more slowly through the gently sloping valley, varying in depth and flow as it passes through bright green grassy banks. The low, tumbling mountains on either side of the Lundarreykjadalur Valley and the lie of the river relative to the path of the sun create varied lighting conditions which challenge the fisherman to alter his tactics on each approach.

Angling enthusiasts come to the Grímsá from all over the world and, once smitten by its charms, tend to return each year. The brilliant American fisherman, Ernest Schweibert, was devoted to the Grímsá and actually designed its rather unique fishing lodge. Another renowned American angler, the conservationist Nathaniel Reed, holds the record for the largest fish caught on a fly, a 27 pounder. (Icelander Halldor Vilhjálmsson caught the 34 pound record in 1917). I have fished the Grímsá River every year for 27 years, always with immeasurable pleasure.

There are over 60 marked fishing spots on the Grímsá, many with names few foreigners would attempt to pronounce, such as Neðri Gullberastaðastrengur. One of the most beautiful and challenging fly fishing pools in all of Iceland has the strange name of Viðbjóður (Nastiness), a name derived from a folk tale about a mutilated fish that was caught there. The river runs between magnificent cliffs over a low waterfall into the pool and flows out in a succession

Late Summer, Top Beat

of smaller, narrow falls. Viðbjóður severely tests the angler's casting skill, and the ability to control the fly's drift through complex currents is essential. Pools in the upper part of the river, such as the Oddstaðafljót, offer a different fishing experience. It is a wide and long, slow-flowing pool with beautiful grass banks under which very deep water usually holds hundreds of salmon in late summer.

Mother Nature's bounty varies from year to year and so too the fishing on the Grímsá. Typically the annual catch is around 1400, but as with all salmon rivers the total fluctuates depending on conditions. This has been especially true in recent years. To me this uncertainty adds an element of anticipation and excitement – success on any fishing trip is never guaranteed. But the pleasure of being out in nature never varies.

Footbridge to Miðberg and Lodge

The Grímsá River Owners Association is devoted to conservation and takes an active role in maintaining good salmon habitat. It used to run its own hatchery. An experiment was conducted on the Grímsá by a group of Americans led by Gardner Grant in 1977-1979 which showed the effectiveness of catch-and-release. The mortality rate for the 859 salmon released was less than 4%, and more than 20% of these fish were caught again. Catch-and-release is now actively encouraged. Ten rods were traditionally allowed until several years ago when the number was decreased to eight. This was a sensible decision that was probably unique for Icelandic rivers.

I hope many fly fisherman will get the opportunity to join me on the Grímsá to experience the idyllic moments this queen of Icelandic salmon rivers can produce.

Einar Benediktsson

Jón Thór casting in Strengir Pool

Cave and Cliff Pools

HAFFJARÐARÁ

Grettir

Stone Pool

Old Bridge Pool

To ME, EVERYTHING IN ICELAND was a surprise, and the Haffjarðará, my first Icelandic river, a double surprise. We are learning that northern maritime places are among the most biologically diverse, but a small river running to the sea seems to concentrate these wonders: the resident trout stay put, the sea run trout dwarf their homebound cousins, and the salmon engage our imaginations with their incompletely understood saga. Upland birds like ptarmigan find their living under the streaking shadows of gyrfalcons while puffins spring straight from their cliffs for their ocean provender. Breeding pairs of rare sea eagles nest on the Snæfellsness Peninsula at whose base the Haffjarðará finds the sea. There's a lot going on in this odd landscape with its modest volcanoes, blunt headlands and stirring North Atlantic skies.

The bottom of the Haffjarðará is tidal, the top drinkable sweet-water springs and a lake made by a lava slide. Meandering in between is a trout fisherman's salmon river that changes speed and circumstance with every yard along moss covered lava banks which yield to fragrant meadows where salmon rest under overhanging grass. In one pool with a falls at its head, salmon are seen throughout, angled in all directions as they face its complex currents. In another, they rise from the dark to intercept your fly. If you are fortunate enough to be guided by an Icelandic scholar, as I was, you learn that this is also an old human place with a rapturous pre-Christian history. One splendid run is named for Grettir, the outlaw-hero of the Sagas who at this point jumped the Haffjarðará, qualifying for the Olympics in any year, but missing the salmon fishing, for Grettir is a profound run that must be taken apart in sections.

All rivers have a defining mood and the mood of the Haffjarðará is cheerful: the bucolic landscape, the healthy stock of sea run fish, and the light human footprint; the world as it should be.

Thomas McGuane

HOFSÁ

THE WORDS OF ONE OF ICELAND'S renowned poet-songwriters give an insight into the intense emotions Hofsá can generate:

"Don't invite me to fish Hofsá if you are only going to ask me to fish it once, for I know I will leave in love, never wishing to fish another river."

To fish Hofsá is to experience Iceland at its best. Whether at the beginning of the season, when the meadows are alive with snipe, plover, whimbrel and redshank and the fisherman must be ever vigilant to aerial attacks from terns and skuas. Or in the languid dog-days of summer, when the midday sun erases shadows from the pools, rendering fishing futile until the shade lengthens and the pools once again come alive. Or at the end of the season, when man, horse and dog muster sheep from the hill while skeins of geese etch the skies leaden with the tinge of autumn. To spend time beside the Hofsá is so much more than fishing – it is to become a part of Iceland and its unique nature.

Odin´s Bank (Beat 1)

The Hofsá is located in the remote northeast of Iceland and the statistics show it to be one of the most prolific rivers in Iceland. It is divided into seven beats, fished one rod per beat with single- or double-handed rods. The 80 named pools spread over 18 km offer fishing that will test the professional and can flatter the beginner. One of the few Icelandic rivers to be "fly only", with mandatory catch-and-release for MSW fish, Hofsá is managed to ensure that there are not only grilse - in abundance, but also a real opportunity to catch a fresh-run 20 pounder.

Smjörfjöll Mountains in background

But facts and figures can tell only a fraction of the story. No graph can ever portray an adrenalin-laced visit to the great Foss, the spectacular natural barrier that marks the top of the Hofsá fishings, clambering down the slope and casting a fly into the narrow, spray-shrouded gorge hoping to hook, play, land and release a fish. No pie chart can ever explain the excitement of spotting for a fishing partner as the fly swings past a fish, helping him make the minute adjustments to the cast and presentation that will brush the fly against the salmon's nose, and then watching as its white maw opens to take it. No spreadsheet will ever show the riffling hitched fly as it tracks across the surface, the bulge in the water as a fish prepares to attack, or the heart-stopping smash of the take. No league table will ever describe an hour-long battle through pools and over rapids ending in a breathless release – and then the time spent on a grassy bank in contented reflection of a job well done. Experiences such as these can be found individually on many Icelandic rivers, but it is only on the Hofsá that they combine so frequently to test, to thrill and, on occasion, to torment the angler.

Here you can catch Hofsá salmon on the fringe of the Arctic Circle in the midst of Nature in all its glory; salmon which are hard won and the stuff of our piscatorial dreams.

The poet was right – to fish the Hofsá once can never be enough.

Sigurður Helgason and Robert Jackson

Burstafell Farm

Black Bank (Beat 5) and Hofsá Lodge beyond

LANGÁ

LANGÁ SALMON ARE SPECIAL. They have adapted over time to deal with the situation that faces them immediately upon entering the river – the high waterfall Skuggafoss, or Shadow Falls, which is less than a kilometer from the sea. Langá salmon are slender and long (like the name of their river, the "Long River"), but their most unique characteristic is a broad tail. This gives them the great speed and powerful leaping ability necessary to shoot themselves out of the water high into the falls or all the way to the brink.

A fish ladder was built years ago at Skuggafoss, but the salmon seem to consider it a necessary test of their fortitude to attack the waterfall. They do so again and again until, finally exhausted, they reluctantly retreat to the easier passage. When a big run of fish is on, you can often see numerous salmon airborne all at once. Even the most fanatic fishermen set their equipment aside to observe this amazing spectacle.

Long ranked among Iceland's best salmon rivers, the Langá normally has substantial salmon runs, with the catch fluctuating somewhat year to year depending on weather and water levels. Catches in recent years have approached and even exceeded 2,000 salmon during the June 20 to September 20 season. Catch statistics for the Langá go back to the earliest days of angling in Iceland. The British fishermen who leased the river during the latter 19th and early 20th centuries kept very detailed catch books and these have been preserved. These ancient records are not really comparative to the statistics kept today, since the fishable portion of the Langá has been lengthened substantially and many fewer rods fished the river in those early days (three rods as opposed to the 12 permitted today), but they do show one very interesting fact – on average approximately half the salmon caught by the early British anglers were multi-sea-winter fish. Today on the Langá, as on most salmon rivers, the percentage of larger MSW salmon is much, much smaller, typically less than 10% of the annual catch.

The Langá's productivity is not accidental – the river has been well cared for over the years. Far up the valley there is another major waterfall, Sveðjufoss, or Hatchet Falls. It was impassable for salmon until a salmon ladder was constructed there in 1967. Those who installed this ladder had no idea if it would work. They were soon rewarded by catching the first salmon above the falls and, overwhelmed by joy, they poured Campari into the pool. This explains the rather unusual name the pool has carried ever since. A reservoir was constructed below the springs which provide much of the water for the

Ingvi Örn Ingvason below Skuggafoss

river. This reservoir now ensures adequate water flow throughout the fishing season, even in time of drought. The fishing is exceptionally accessible, with well maintained farm roads along most of its length.

The Langá is not a big river and wading is usually not a problem, but fishing it does have its complications. The water is usually crystal-clear and it can be difficult to entice salmon to bite, especially in full sun light. The solution is often found in using micro flies and delicate line. The riffling hitch works well in a number of spots, producing a spectacular show when a salmon rises from the depths and charges wildly for the fly. Langá salmon generally weigh in the range of 4-6 pounds, but quite a few weightier fish are caught each year. While the salmon typically are not giants, their oversized tails generate fantastic strength and stamina. Fishermen are usually surprised on landing a fish that it is not the much bigger salmon they thought they had hooked. The old adage, "it's not the size of the fish in the fight, but the size of the fight in the fish", is appropriate on the Langá.

The surroundings of the Langá are varied and beautiful, with grassy dales and bushes framing the river. There are low gravel banks, comfortable for walking, and several small but spectacular canyons that call for the angler to proceed with caution. In the upper valley above Sveðjufoss there is no human habitation, leaving the visitor in perfect solitude with only the sounds of the river and birds. No time of day is more beautiful on the Langá than sunset, when the sun sinks into the ocean over the horizon and a golden glow settles over the glacier-topped volcano Snæfellsjökull in the distance. This is a view no one can forget, nor is it ever easy to leave behind.

Steinar J. Lúðvíksson

Myrkhylur

View of Shelter from Langá Lodge

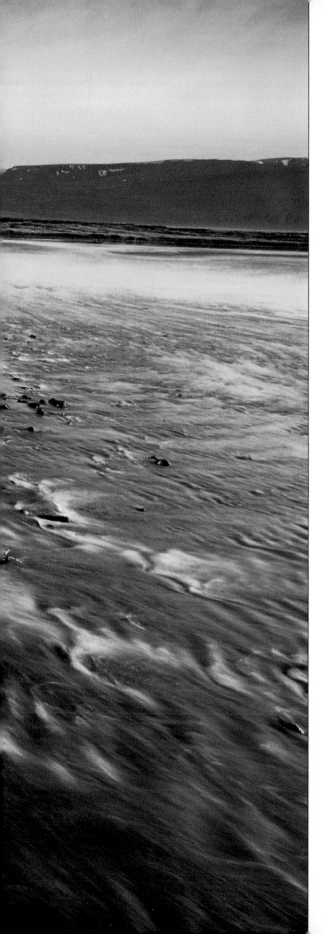

LAXÁ IN AÐALDAL

Iceland has only one big Laxá and that's the Laxá in Aðaldal. How well it deserves that title! The country's second largest non-glacial river is big and awesome as it thunders over the five spillways that breach the imposing Æðarfossar cliff just metres from tidal water. The salmon ascend its three lesser torrents.

All five of the cataracts plunge into productive angling pools but they are turbulent and snag-strewn and set amongst precipitous paths, wildflower-decked islets and the debris of ancient rock falls. A hooked salmon invariably tries to return to the sea and has to be chased through a veritable tank-trap of obstacles and side channels. As one of Iceland's best anglers said to me: "This must be the most exciting place in the world to catch a salmon." And it probably is!

Above the falls the river is much more sedate. But everywhere the Big Laxá produces big fish. Salmon over 20 pounds and brown trout of 5-10 pounds are fairly common. Large numbers of magnificent fish, however, are not the Laxá's greatest contribution to salmon angling. Its great achievement is to have inspired the conservation activities of a man named Orri Vigfússon.

Orri and his cousin, Ingvi Hrafn Jónsson, both born not far from the Big Laxá in July 1942, began their salmon angling careers on the river and have fished it for over 40 years. The joy of fishing this wonderful river gave them their deep devotion to the Atlantic salmon. Then came the commercial fishing slaughter that followed the discovery of the salmon's main sea feeding grounds off Greenland and the Faroes.

By 1989 Orri and Ingvi were so concerned at the steep decline in salmon stocks everywhere that they persuaded their angling friends to join them in launching the North Atlantic Salmon Fund. Both men made significant personal financial commitments to underwrite NASF's work.

Since then Orri has worked tirelessly to turn the North Atlantic into a salmon sanctuary and at last numbers are rebuilding. So all salmon anglers should thank the Laxá for inspiring its two greatest admirers to undertake this enormous challenge.

Æðarfossar (Beat 1)

I went to Northern Iceland to see why the Big Laxá has cast such an enduring spell over two otherwise hard-headed Icelandic businessmen. I soon understood. The Big Laxá is a river for all seasons. The Arctic Circle is less than 40 km from its mouth and winter batters the river with storms, snow and ice. It is a quite different place in the short Icelandic summer. Fringed by snow-capped mountains, the fertile valley is usually snug and warm. But when the wind swings north and the sun turns its back, the angler feels the chill breath of the Norse gods and is thankful he brought his thermals!

The 58 km of the Big Laxá divides itself into three districts of great challenge to the fly fisher. From its outflow from Lake Mývatn, it hurries north as the Laxá in Mývatnssveit - one of the world's best trout rivers. Splitting between islands, reuniting, widening to 400 metres in some areas and narrowing into tight channels in others, this section is spectacularly productive. Over 4,000 of its ferociously strong trout are taken each year.

When it becomes the Laxá in Laxárdalur it remembers its dignity. Fly only and restricted to fewer anglers, it is still stuffed with wild trout and yields another 2,000 or so annually.

Below lies the Laxá in Aðaldalur, home of the big salmon. The 25 km to the sea are headed by a hydropower station, built in 1939 on falls the salmon never could climb. The hydro men inserted a fish ladder, but the salmon still refuse to invade the trout territory. The 18 salmon beats below the dam averaged 1,800 fish a year before a temporary fluctuation of marine conditions depressed smolt survival off Iceland's north coast. Happily, the runs are rebuilding.

My visit did not disappoint. The Laxá, with its clear waters, pure air, remarkable bird life and fertile, volcanic scenery, is spectacular. The pools are masterpieces of nature, as if specially designed for fly fishers. It is mostly easy wading. All around is a patchwork of colour - red-roofed farmsteads, green pastures, a plethora of wild flowers and areas of black lava carved by wind and frost into bizarre shapes.

For over 1,100 years the Laxá has fed and watered its farmers. Now they thrive on a financial cornucopia created by anglers. Two-thirds of the season is rightly reserved for Icelanders, so competition for the remaining places is fierce. If you can find a vacancy, grab it! And include the Dimmblá, Black Sheep and Frances in your fly box – in what may seem ridiculously small sizes. If they fail, try a 15 cm Collie Dog or Sunray Shadow.

Michael Charleston

Sasa Savic on Beat 3

Heiðarendi (Beat 2)

Mjósund (Beat 2 above Æðarfossar)

Page 61: Øystein Aas at Mjósund (Beat 2)

LAXÁ IN KJÓS

FLOWING IN ALL ITS DIVERSITY through an ever changing terrain only a few miles north of Reykjavík, the Laxá in Kjós is enchanting. The uppermost beat is quite mystical. At every turn, the magnificent landscape is interwoven with the ancient folklore of trolls, elves and giants.

The Laxá flows 16 miles from Lake Stíflísdalsvatn to the sea. Through the years much has been done to improve the spawning grounds and clear the way for salmon to run up as far as the Þórufoss, an impassable waterfall a short distance from the river's source. In 1974 a new fish-ladder was opened to enable salmon to bypass the Laxfoss, and less than five years ago alterations were done on the Pokafoss for this purpose.

The hallmark of the Laxá in Kjós is the diversity of its fishing beats. Just below Þórufoss it flows through deep gorges. Then it changes into smaller waterfalls, rapids and pools. This magnificent interplay of nature is a great bonus to salmon fishing and here the angler is alone in his own world. Further downstream, the river winds romantically through the countryside between meadows and fields. This is the middle section. Here one must approach with the utmost care so as not to spook the fish. The river is very calm and clear, and the salmon is wary to every movement. Anglers are sometimes seen kneeling a bit back from the stream when casting. The fisherman who has learned how to be successful on this beat can be truly said to have graduated from "Salmon Fishing University"!

Just above the Laxfoss the only tributary which carries salmon joins the main river, the Bugða. It originates in Lake Meðalfellsvatn and flows for a little less than two miles, a neat and very nice salmon fishing stream. The most popular pool is Hornhylur, which usually holds a large number of salmon. The fish can run all the way up the Bugða and in the fall quite a number are caught in the lake itself. The catchment area of Laxá in Kjós and Bugða is more than 77 square miles. In the middle of the valley between the two rivers, Mount Meðalfell thrusts up to tower over the countryside in all its grandeur.

The lowest beat of the Laxá begins at Laxfoss and ends in the estuary. Here you have one great fishing spot after another and anglers can fish two different pools standing side by side. The river begins to rush to the sea through rapids, small waterfalls and fast water with calmer glides in between. When a big

Gylfi Gautur below Þórufoss

run is on, the whole series of pools seems to seethe with salmon. Just before it joins the sea, the river unfolds in the so-called Höklar, a challenging stretch where it can be difficult to avoid falling on slippery rocks when fighting a newly run salmon.

Möðruvallaeyrar

The Laxá in Kjós is well suited for fishing with small flies and employing a variety of differing techniques. Well known patterns such as Green Braham, Collie Dog, Hairy Mary, Blue Charm and Black Sheep in sizes 10-14 work well. Hitch tubes and micro tubes can also lead to success, especially in black and blue. In early summer and floods, Red and Black Frances tube flies are a good choice.

The river is very productive, and in 1988 a new record was set with 3860 salmon. The first runs come in early June, but most of the salmon usually run the first two weeks of July. By then all fishing spots are active and you are not likely to find a more enjoyable and varied salmon fishing experience anywhere in the world.

Þórarinn Sigþórsson

Streamside Freshet

Klingenberg

LAXÁ IN LEIRÁRSVEIT

ONE OF MY MOST MEMORABLE losses took place years ago in this small and beautiful river - in pool 11 known as Sunnefjufoss. I can still see the big salmon in my mind's eye - it grows bigger year after year - swimming in the clear whirling water below the falls while I desperately tried to get down from the high cliff from where I had rashly and inconsiderately tried a few casts. The fish had taken my fly, and I had to get down to the water. I jumped an abyss I would never have dared attempt had it not been for the fish, which had come out into the quiet waters in the little bend of the river below the falls. Miraculously I survived the jump, still with a tight line and a struggling fish on the other end, and then started to scramble down rubble with small stones which sliced into my waders. But then, only a few yards from the bank, the fish quietly spat out my fly and disappeared in the direction of the sphinx-shaped cliffs called Ljónið. Every year since I have visited that place, remembering that magnificent fish and shuddering at the sight of those cliffs.

But Laxá in Leirársveit also holds memories of many beautiful fish caught, and landed. At Miðfellsfljót near the road to Svínadalur I caught three on the

Miðfellslfljót

Fast water along Jónsstrengir

67

same small fly, before number four ran away with it - a microtube I got from a policeman in the airport when I landed, sparsely tied with a few black hairs and a twist of silver. "Try this," he said, "it comes from this guy," gesturing at the big friendly Labrador sniffing for hash in the arriving luggage. He then petted his rear quarters, and the dog took a big leap, with a suspicious and reproachful look on his face. The dog obviously remembered having his small hairs plucked – but the fly worked great!

It is a wonderful and peaceful place - if you do not approach too close to the nests of the arctic terns. They warn you with the shrill cries that give the bird its name - kría! kría! - and then attack you in daring dives. I call them "Polish Cavalry" - their fearless and reckless behavior reminding me of the brave men who attacked German tanks on horseback at the beginning of WW II.

This river is relatively small, you'll get to know it in a few days. The run from Eyrarvatn to the sea is short, but it offers a lot of differing water and landscapes – from the upper river with its dramatic falls that the fish now ascend by fish ladder, to the long and peaceful stretches closer to the snug lodge downstream. Laxá in Leirársveit is a wonderful place to return to, because you feel immediately at home.

One year I caught absolutely nothing for the better part of a week. I knew it would be like that when I arrived. The sun was baking and the scent of freshly cut grass was intoxicating, but it was also the smell of defeat. You could see all the big salmon, slowly moving up the warm river, but you could not sell them even the fanciest flies. It says a lot about the qualities of the Laxá in Leirársveit that even this experience remains a warm and happy memory.

Uffe Ellemann-Jensen

Redshank

Kattarfoss

NORÐURÁ

THE NORÐURÁ ("NORTH RIVER") is one of the great rivers of Iceland. Rich in history, it offers a unique and royal fishing experience in a spectacular setting, hence its nickname "Queen of Rivers".

Located in the Borgarfjörður area of the western part of Iceland, it originates in the mountainous region of Holtavörðuheiði, where the mountains stretch their snow-capped peaks towards the clear heavens. A flat-topped ridge of mountains rises to the east and to the west is the stark triangular bulk of a volcano. This is classic Icelandic landscape – barren, rugged, perhaps even somewhat frightening, but strikingly beautiful.

The first small streams of the Norðurá trickle from a small mountain lake, and start the journey towards the Atlantic Ocean through a landscape of gnarled lava carpeted in soft luminous green "grimmia". Almost 60 km later the Norðurá, by then a large river, joins the even larger Hvítá, whose name "white" is derived from the glacier melt that colours it. Six km further west of this confluence the flow of the combined rivers (which at this point also include the Grímsá and the Þverá Kjarrá) meet the ocean.

It is hard to find a river offering more variety of fishing. There are more than 100 named pools along its length. In the upper part one finds small pools and challenging spots where the fisherman must be careful when he approaches the river. A bit further downriver are slow moving water and deep holding pools, where the salmon are just waiting for a small riffling hitched Green Highlander or a fast stripped Blue Charm #16. In the lower part there is an abundance of large and smooth pools. And then there is Eyrin, one of the most elegant pools in all of Iceland. Fishing it is an experience that cannot be adequately described. As a typical arterial river, the Norðurá is usually sapphire blue. In heavy rains, it might turn emerald green and cloudy, challenging to the fisherman but always exciting.

The Norðurá is one of the most productive rivers in Iceland, with fish runs having actually improved since netting on the Hvítá was terminated in 1991. One of the first rivers to open in Iceland, the Norðurá is fished from the first of June. Aggressive runs of two-year salmon arrive in early June. Beginning at the end of June and continuing during the first two weeks of July, huge runs of grilse fill the river, attacking everything in sight. The grilse run is best fished with light tackle, a floating line and small, elegant flies – an appealing prospect to most anglers. Few could resist the temptation to drift a small Red

Frances across crystal waters, with dark volcanoes and lava behind you, the green blaze of mountains in front and the prospect of a silver fish fresh from the ocean in every pool.

The Reykjavík Angling Club has leased the river for the past 60 years, but provides access to non-members, both local fishermen and sportsmen from abroad, and comfortable accommodation in its lodge. Some of its guests have become totally smitten with the river, like the famous Capt. Aspinall who first fished the Norðurá in the 1930's and has been seen every summer since then, fishing his favourite Myrkhylur (Dark Pool) where he caught a 36 pounder in 1932.

Bjarni Júlíusson

Icelandic Pony

Glitstaðir Pool

SELÁ

THE SELÁ IS SO BRILLIANTLY gin-clear that at times one can imagine there is no water between the angler and his quarry. The colors and patterning of stones at the bottom of a 10 or 12 feet deep pool are as clear as if they lay at the angler's feet. As a bonus, the water is so pure that if the fisherman is thirsty he can dip down a hand and drink straight from the river. The Selá is my favorite river for fishing the riffling hitch. Probably because of the clarity of the water, the fish respond to this exciting method remarkably often, and the big fish fall for it just as readily as the grilse.

The Selá is a river of fascinating variety. There are flat pools and tumbling waterfalls, deep pools and shallow glides, gravelly runs and stunning canyons. Every one of them presents the angler with new challenges. These multiple flows give the angler plenty to think about. In fact, there is more to the diversity of this river than most people can absorb in just one visit.

The Selá is very fortunate because it has a very stable flow of crystalline water and a seemingly inexhaustible supply of ideal spawning gravel. Visiting anglers go away with everlasting memories of the quality of sport the Selá has given them and of the great beauty of this remote part of Northeast Iceland. Remember that this is the real stuff – wilderness fishing for totally wild salmon in an unspoiled natural environment.

The Selá is an outstanding example of what proper salmon conservation can do and would serve admirably as a model for many less fortunate rivers. The principal objective of those who work for the Selá and watch over its progress is an abundance of adult fish, and with common sense management, that is exactly what they have achieved.

Not many years ago difficult falls confined the spawning mostly to Selá's lower reaches. Luckily, my fishing partner, Vífill Oddsson, a leading authority on the design and building of fish passes, designed a fish pass that the fish readily use. Today salmon can easily travel upriver for 28 km. Apart from an extensive and hugely valuable increase in spawning territory, the additional water now provides excellent sport for a good many extra angling rods.

When the Strengur Syndicate first leased the river in 1969 the annual average catch was about 170 salmon. The syndicate thought carefully before deciding on the phases of an improvement policy and then set about the introduction of several schemes that have greatly increased the river's salmon stocks and

Long stretch of upper Selá

angling catches. This includes the buying out of nets, the building of the fish ladder, the introduction of strict limits on the number of fish that can be killed, the popularization of catch-and-release and the support of sanctuary agreements that reach out to the salmon feeding grounds. This worked so well that the catches grew steadily, and the rods were soon landing 600 salmon a year. Despite the sad decline in salmon numbers in so many other places, the last decade has seen that figure increase to a yearly catch of 1,000 to 1,300 salmon. At the beginning of the new millennium the annual tally reached the 1,600 mark and for the last two years was around 2,500, or roughly 15 times what it was when Strengur first leased the river.

Orri Vigfússon

George H.W. Bush at Fossbrot

"It is impossible to describe the wonders of fishing the Selá, an astoundingly beautiful river. The fish, fresh from the sea, are strong fighters and remarkably beautiful. My whole experience in Iceland was very special and a real joy."

George H.W. Bush

Max Gloor selecting fly

ÞVERÁ KJARRÁ

THE ÞVERÁ AND KJARRÁ ARE in fact the same stream, originating in Iceland's north-western highlands. The landowners call the entire stream Þverá or "Branch River", while those doing the fishing call the upper stretches Kjarrá or Bush River. The river stretches 90 km from its confluence with the glacial Hvítá River up to an altitude of 400 m, but there are no obstacles to block the salmon. Posts in the riverbank identify just under 200 fishing pools, from the lowest down near the Hvítá to the highest far up where the headwaters flow out of countless ponds and lakes. Many of these pools bear English as well as Icelandic names, like Five Pools, Hambro, Three Princesses, Canyon, Green Pool, Hell Gate and Stewart, reflecting the English fishermen who first fished the river over 100 years ago.

The lower river is characterized by lush farm fields of bright green grass and brilliant yellow buttercups, later on exuding the smell of fresh hay drying in the sun, and cows lazily chewing cud along the bank. Under their placid, indifferent gaze, the angler assumes the same calm, though pools such as the legendary Klapparfljót hold 20 pound salmon that can violently bring a change in mood.

Upstream, the canyons and pools of the Kjarrádalur valley and the gravel flats still higher up have an abundance of unmarked, constantly changing fishing sites untouched by human habitation. Beyond the road end, there are only faint tracks left by fishing vehicles. Here one fishes in perfect solitude, with a snowy white glacier dome above you and a triangular volcano in the distance.

Fishing vehicle at Örnólfsdalur

Lower Johnson Pool

So close to the Arctic Circle, the brightness of the sky is pure and lasting. Mornings are crisp. Every creature understands these conditions are fleeting and savours them in full. The birds fly frantically back and forth to feed their chicks, the ewes bleat at their new-born lambs, leading them further and further into the moors as the summer progresses, and the salmon run up to their native pools to spawn. Drawn to this beauty, I raise my prayer to the river:

Kjarrá river, cool and bright,
Come deliver pleasure.
Let me shiver, line be tight;
I love your giving treasure!

Lupine

"Being outdoors is good for bankers," a seven year old boy once told me. His simple but profound words have stayed with me. Worldly cares dissipate and the mind becomes at peace in the unblemished natural beauty of a river. And the rhythms of the salmon fisherman, casting, mending the line, holding it steady and pulling it in, then moving down and repeating this ritual again and again, are mesmerising. But no, suddenly the fly is grabbed away! The perpetrator is strong and confident, fully intend on his purpose. Abruptly the angler experiences a full range of emotions: joy, hope, excitement, doubt, trepidation, and sometimes disappointment. The disappointments keep our interest from ever fading.

The Þverá Kjarrá boast some of the highest catches of Icelandic rivers - an average of 1,800 to 2,000 salmon annually, once peaking as high as 4000. Some sections of the Kjarrá are physically challenging, tucked into narrow channels, gorges and even canyons, and can only be reached on foot by scrambling up and down steep banks. Fortunately there is a wealth of excellent fishing spots that are easy to reach and fish.

Selstrengur

The river tends to run low in late July, when the whopper salmon, which typically arrive early in the season, become lackadaisical. Grilse, however, keep running, astonishing people who catch them in the uppermost reaches covered with sea lice. These fish have swum some 90 km within the short 48 hour period that sea lice can stay on in fresh water. Low water calls for small sized 10-14 flies and tiny micro tubes. Some favourites are the Stoat's Tail, Green Butt, Collie Dog, Nighthawk, Blue Charm, Hairy Mary, Munro Killer, Thunder & Lightning, Jock Scott and Black and Red Frances.

When evening comes, there is no better place than in the lodge with one's favourite aperitif and a group of good friends delivering their report on the day's fishing. This is my home, and sharing the experience of this great river with friends is my greatest joy.

Ragnar Önundarson

Brúartangi

Berghylur Pool with Norðtunga Farm and Baula Mountain beyond

VATNSDALSÁ

LOVE OF THE VATNSDALSÁ ("Lake Valley River") and the beautiful valley from which it takes its name runs deep in my family. My father was born on its banks and in my boyhood I spent summers on the farm where he was brought up, and there first experienced the thrill of catching fish when I was allowed to join the farmers drag netting for salmon and trout. Later in life, after I had become addicted to salmon fishing, I fished there regularly for many years and learned to appreciate it as one of the most outstanding fly fishing waters in Iceland.

The fishable part of the Vatnsdalsá flows north approximately 30 km from an impassable falls, the Dalfoss, through narrow valley walls in the upper reaches down into wider pools as it reaches its outflow on a large tidal lagoon which it shares with the Laxá in Ásum. It is a classic Icelandic salmon river with an excellent variety of pools.

The fascinating history of the Vatnsdalsá goes back eleven centuries. The old Sagas tell of a fight over fishing rights that broke out between the sons of Ingimundur the Old, the leader of the first settlers of the valley, and a quarrelsome neighbor on the opposite side of the river. Ingimundur tried to separate the battling foes but was hit by a spear and fatally wounded. To avoid making matters worse, he hid his wound and managed to ride back to his house. Before he died he sent a messenger to warn the neighbor of what had happened so that he could make his escape. In the old Sagas noble gestures often go unrewarded. So it was with Ingimundur's kind act – the neighbor got away but Ingimundur's sons later caught up with him and avenged their father's death. Ingimundur the Old has been revered by the people of the valley ever since.

Fishing on the Vatnsdalsá was somewhat more peaceful over the following 1000 years, and useful in providing food for the locals. In 1936 the river's superb qualities as an angler's paradise was recognized by an Englishman, Mr. Lionel Fortescue. He leased the fishing rights for 15 years which helped persuade the farmers to cease their netting which was seriously depleting the salmon stock. The farmers' faith in Mr. Fortescue was not misplaced. Aside from being a keen and skilled angler, he was a passionate conservationist whose prime interest was to restore the depleted salmon stock and make the river more attractive to fishermen. He released many of the fish he caught, which was regarded as very bizarre behavior at that time.

View towards Skriðuvað and Hnausastrengur Pools

Mr. Fortescue was a classics master at Eton and, as a young student in London during WW II, I visited him there and helped him write a long letter in Icelandic to a well-known naturalist in Iceland in which he proposed ways to improve salmon runs in the river. His devotion to conservation and the Vatnsdalsá was certainly a major factor in making it one of the most delightful rivers to fish in Iceland. He would be happy to know that half a century later the Vatnsdalsá became the first salmon river in Iceland where catch-and-release has been made obligatory.

Jóhannes Nordal

Vivvi Orrason preparing to fish Hólakvörn

Upper Pools Rofabakki, Ármót, Álka and Grjóthrúgukvörn

VÍÐIDALSÁ

Summers are short near the arctic circle – far too short for passionate anglers who have waited through the long, dark days of winter for the ice and snow to melt and for nature to come to life once more. When summer does arrive, it starts with zeal, as June brings light throughout the night as well as day. The sun barely slips below the horizon, and then only for a few moments, gathering energy for the next lengthy day. During those moments all nature holds its breath – the wind quietens, birds rest with head under wing, and the grass stays motionless so as not to lose even a dew drop.

Rolling grandly between its banks, the Víðidalsá ("Willow Bush River") flows through grassy farming areas. Broad, shallow expanses with a calm, steady current are interspersed by more unpredictable rapids here and there. This is just what the fly fishing enthusiast calls for, where the most telling fishing rig consists of a floating line and a tiny fly that just ripples the surface. With one's eyes glued to the fly, its every drift seems to last an eternity. Does any flash or disturbance reveal a chasing fish? Has a salmon taken the fly? Yes! Now count to two and respond to the bite.

Although the valley farms look ordinary, history lies everywhere. Around 900, the family of Auðun Skökull claimed this valley and settled here. He was an ancestor of a British monarch. In the 14th century, a farmer by the banks of this river decided to have the histories of Nordic kings and land exploration recorded – a tremendous feat requiring the skins of 113 calves, but yielding a book that is now one of the leading references on medieval Nordic history.

Around a thousand salmon per year are caught in the Víðidalsá. Renowned for offering large salmon, its pride is the biggest one caught on a fly in Iceland during the latter part of the 20th century, weighing over 35 pounds. Having known this river's reputation from childhood, the anticipation I felt when I finally had the prospect of fishing there became almost unbearable. Nor did the river disappoint me upon first acquaintance – the goddess of fishing, in the form of big female salmon, flirted with my flies among the ripples, and I was sold to the Víðidalsá forever.

The Víðidalsá by no means harbours salmon only. August brings runs of Arctic char, numbering in the thousands, and by October the swarms of char

Stekkjarfljót Pool in uppermost Víðidalsá

87

that slither to spawn via shallows and up into the very shallowest of brooks and calm spots are a magnificent sight.

Fossar Rapids in lower river

The ancient poetry of Völuspá, telling the story of the earth's creation from a heathen perspective, could just as well have been inspired on the banks of the Víðidalsá:

> "...She sees Earth rise up once more,
> Out of the sea, lively green.
> Sees waterfalls, an eagle soaring -
> That fisherman of the mountains."

Andri Teitsson

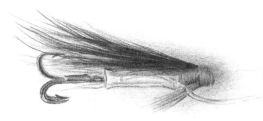

Efri and Neðri Valhylur (Upper and Lower Falcon Pools) in upper river

IRELAND

Bann

Foyle

NORTHERN
IRELAND   Belfast

Moy

Boyne

REPUBLIC
OF
IRELAND

Dublin

Blackwater

Dunluce Castle ruins at mouth of the Bann

BANN (LOWER)

ALTHOUGH ITS NAME SUGGESTS OTHERWISE, the Lower Bann lies to the north of Lough Neagh, the largest freshwater lake in the British Isles into which drains the greater part of Northern Ireland. Six major rivers flow into Lough Neagh, including the Moyola, Ballinderry, Six Mile Water, Maine and Upper Bann, all of which offer fine salmon and trout fishing.

As the only outflow to the sea from Lough Neagh, the Lower Bann is a mighty river. It runs for about 60 km from its outlet on the Lough to its estuary below Coleraine. Unusually the river does not run close to main roads but the railway from Belfast to Coleraine is often near at hand and this setting is such that it has been described by Michael Palin as one of the great train journeys of the world.

Movanagh Beat

In its heyday the Lower Bann was the equal of any Atlantic salmon river in the world. Tales are still told of the netting station at the Crannagh, where tractors had to be employed at the height of the season to haul nets so full of fish that they could not be pulled by hand. Well within living memory catches of 100 grilse per day were recorded on its best beats, with an occasional two-sea-winter salmon added for good measure.

The famous pool of Carnroe

Like many major rivers in Ireland, large sections of the Lower Bann were dredged in the 1920's and turned into virtual canals for the purposes of drainage and navigation. Right up until 1960, Lough Neagh itself was still in a pristine state, virtually unchanged over the millennia. Sadly this is not the case today with the ravages of the EU Common Agricultural Policy and population growth all too evident in the highly eutrophic state of the Lough and river.

A few sections of the original river remain, such as the famous beats of Carnroe, Movanagher and Portna, all of which still receive excellent runs of summer grilse. In spite of increasing levels of smolt mortality at sea in recent years, runs into the Bann of around 8000 fish per year have been holding steady. Magic salmon fishing is still very much on and the knowledgeable angler can expect to catch several grilse in a day on these beats in July.

What does the future hold? We are already reaping the benefits of both the cessation of commercial fishing on the Bann itself and the buy out of the draft nets off the North Coast. Farming policy has turned away from maximization of output at any cost and the Water Framework Directive now holds out a real prospect of improvement in water quality. Habitat restoration and improvement programs are being carried out by the angling clubs who lease the fishing on the rivers feeding into the Lough, where most spawning takes place. A major restoration program, the "Healthy River Plan", designed to coordinate restoration effort across the entire Bann system is gathering momentum.

One of my fondest memories of the Bann was fishing with my father-in-law one morning in July. The old man had stopped fishing himself, but always came along for the day, sat on the bank and passed judgement on the proceedings. It was a "red letter" day for me – in about an hour and a half I had caught and returned six grilse straight from the ocean. On returning to shore, I asked the old man what he thought. "Aye, disappointing" was his reply.

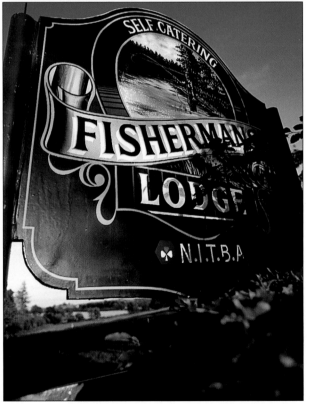

What it must it have been like when he was a lad! What it could be again if we commit ourselves to making our dream into reality.

David Agnew

Along the Lower Bann

BLACKWATER

THE RIVER IS A FLOWING CHRONICLE from the misty mountains of County Kerry, where it rises, to its mouth at Youghal, 160-odd km by water from source to sea, carrying the ebbs and flows of Irish history down through the ages.

The Gaelic Irish called it *Abhainn Mhoir*, the big river. The English settlers looked at its colour, darkened by the sediment from the peat bogs of Kerry, and gave it the name it carries today. Perhaps it was not only the colour that influenced them, but also the river's foul mood in winter or early spring when a flood could carry away all in its path – trees, bridges and even people. Summer brings a marked transformation. The river flows gently through rich farming valleys, past great houses and Norman castles of the ancient province of Munster, below ivied stone bridges and past prosperous towns that are the symbols of the rich Ireland of the 21st Century.

Lismore Castle

History is enriched along the Blackwater's run through Kerry, across north Cork into Waterford, then back into Cork to the beautiful south coast of Ireland. Go to the little village of Killavullen. It sits on the stretch of the

Top Flat Pool

Blackwater I know best, and you will probably conclude that no person of interest ever lived in this isolated place. The signs point you to the birthplace of Nano Nagle, the founder of the Presentation Sisters order of nuns, a piece of history that may not strike every visitor with awe. Yet Edmund Burke, one of the greatest statemen of 18th Century Europe, spent his childhood here, and the Hennessy family, Gaelic aristocrats who sailed to France to fight for a French king rather than serve an English monarch, were born here and keep their links to this day, in spite of centuries of separation and a fortune gained from their cognac.

A few miles across country is Doneraile, through which flows the Blackwater's tributary, the Awbeg ("Little River"). There Edmund Spenser lived and wrote *The Faerie Queene*, to the delight of his friend Sir Walter Raleigh who lived on his own Munster estate while Mayor of Youghal. Go downriver on the Blackwater and you come to one of the most productive and concentrated fisheries in Ireland, where Clondulane Weir slows the upward migration of the salmon. On a bluff above the weir is Careysville House. It belongs to the Duke of Devonshire, as does Lismore Castle further downriver. One of the Duke's forebears placed a cricket pavilion on the bank to use as a fishing hut. It stands there to this day.

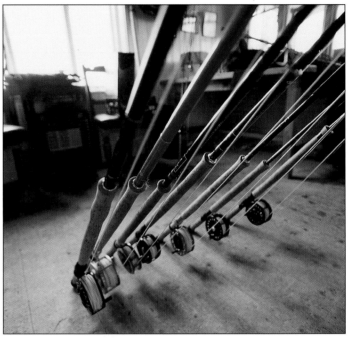

Rods in waiting

A few miles from Careysville is Fermoy, the town from which the Black-and-Tans regiment raided the wild country of West Cork in Britain's attempt to foil Cork's heroes of the Irish Independence movement, Michael Collins and Tom Barry, who carried the Munster spirit of armed insurrection forward after the collapse of the Easter Rising in Dublin in 1916, and won:

"A country rising from its knees / To upset all the histories."

The Blackwater's moods continue to swing as history did, and so do its fortunes. It was, not long ago, the migratory home of some of the biggest salmon in Europe. Sportsmen came from far places to fish wonderful fly water, and long mysterious pools where the willows whisper to the angler. They saw the beauty of the river, its little wooded islands, and the Norman keeps built as sentinels on the bluffs above. Its fame spread until it rivalled the Spey and Tweed. Disease struck in the 1960's. The river partly recovered in the 1980's and 1990's, although the big spring fish did not return in strength. The offshore drift nets, a scandal that shamed Ireland for so long, took their toll, reducing the salmon population to a fraction of what it had once been. These terrible nets are banned at last, and I do not think they will return. Hope returns to the river. Perhaps the Blackwater has entered a new chapter of its history, and the great salmon runs will come again.

Padraic Fallon

Cricket pavilion turned into fishing hut

Near Careysville

BOYNE

In ANCIENT TIMES IN IRELAND rivers were revered as goddesses and were the subject of many tales of mystery and imagination. The river I have chosen – with nostalgia – to commemorate, the Boyne (from the name of the goddess, Bóinn), is one of the most famous. It has a particular association with the story of how the great warrior-hero, Finn, acquired his renowned wisdom.

Brian Hegarty at Trim Castle

As a young trainee, Finn was working on the banks of the Boyne for a druid, Aengus, who had spent a lifetime fishing hopefully for the "Salmon of Knowledge". Left alone one day to oversee the cooking of a fish the druid had caught, Finn turned the fish over by hand and then sucked his thumb to relieve the burning pain. Great was his surprise and delight to find that this simple reflex could thenceforth be relied on to open the gates of wisdom. The vexation of the old druid on finding his lifelong dream realized by a mere apprentice is no doubt shared by the practiced angler who sees a novice take over and catch the fish that eluded his expert efforts.

Below Killearin Bridge

For me the Boyne is a river of memories. I grew up in Drogheda, a town of medieval origins near the mouth of the Boyne and some 50 km north of Dublin, on the east coast. Aged about seven, I cycled with my mother along a path that led to grilles across the river which, at permitted times, could be lowered to block the ascent of salmon and enable them to be hauled aboard leather-bound coracles of immemorial origin. Here, I tried surreptitiously to hook a salmon with a hazel rod, a line of twine and a bent pin!

It was fascinating to watch draft nets being paid out at certain points on the river, waiting in suspense for the final heave to the shore, counting the catch of bright silver fish – many of them nine kilos in weight – and wincing as they received the last rites, the blow on the head from the so-called wooden "priest".

Late every autumn, the tree-lined sweep of the Boyne above Oldbridge became a multi-colored splendor. In those boyhood days – before the "prison gates" began to close – one could experience Wordsworthian intimations sitting on the stump of the obelisk commemorating the victory of William of Orange at the 1690 Battle of the Boyne, or peering down the cold passage of the great Stone Age monument at Newgrange, a passage so oriented and designed as to be illuminated by the first rays of the winter solstice. There were reminders along the whole course of the Boyne of the antiquity and beauty of a hinterland containing the most impressive prehistoric monuments on the fringe of Europe and sites associated with the coming of Christianity to Ireland.

Alas, the salmon is no longer an image associated with the Boyne, nor is wisdom a quality to be associated with management of this unique natural resource. To save the wild salmon of the Boyne and other Irish rivers from extinction will require much more effective measures of conservation than have hitherto been applied.

T.K. Whitaker

View towards Slane Bridge

FOYLE

FOR A SALMON ANGLER, few places reflect the changing seasons and passing years better than a favourite salmon pool. I am fortunate to have lived most of my life a few minutes from such a place on the River Mourne, part of the Foyle river system. Here the famous Snaa Pool is formed by the junction of the rivers Mourne and Derg. Below rough white water at their meeting, the combined flow has cut a deep and narrow channel close to the tree-lined bank opposite the hut. Fish lie in large numbers throughout its hundred yards length. Below, the river flows quietly, wide and deep under mature trees on either bank. It is a timeless place of great tranquillity and beauty.

Snaa Beat

Arriving at the pool, the first thing one sees is an isolated mitre shaped rock a few yards from the bank. We use it to gauge river levels, as have generations of anglers before us. Nowadays, the facing side is painted white, calibrated with feet and inches marked in black. The rock has witnessed countless angling dramas, and played a leading role in some. It gives those who fish there much pleasure as a constant frame of reference, like an old friendship that has stood the test of time.

Dr. Alan Hutchison on Snaa Beat

The excitement of arriving at the pool on an early summer's morning never palls, particularly with a falling river and two feet or less showing on the rock, suggesting that fresh fish may have entered the pool overnight. A jumping fish and urgent swirls brings certainty.

I find the fishing completely absorbing. Wading, casting or unravelling a tangled leader are the incidental activities directed at a single objective, presenting the right fly to the right place at the correct pace. Then, like a tug on the chain of a plug, a fish takes the fly. The achievement of this reward requires total concentration, and the mind takes a welcome holiday from more weighty, worldly problems.

The great salmon rivers of the British Isles have long marked national and other political boundaries. So too the Foyle system, with its lower reaches forming the border between Northern Ireland and the Irish Republic and upper parts in both countries. At Strabane the tidal Foyle divides into two main stems, the Mourne and the Finn. Above its junction with the Derg by Newtownstewart, the Mourne becomes the Strule, draining most of County Tyrone in Northern Ireland. The Finn catchment area is in County Donegal in the Republic. These lovely rivers all run through beautiful pastoral countryside, providing the angler an oasis within an oasis.

In the 1960's the Foyle system enjoyed huge runs of salmon and grilse. An average of more than 100,000 fish were taken annually by commercial nets alone during this decade. This netting had the predictable consequences, but the river system still has some of the most prolific runs in the country, with an average declared rod catch of 6,563 for the years 2002-4.

The fishery as a whole is managed by the Loughs Agency, which has the difficult job of trying to accommodate the interests of both sides of the political divide. Recently introduced conservation measures and proposed initiatives are cause for cautious optimism. Surely a Foyle system with salmon runs like those of 50 years ago, making it once more among the most prolific salmon fisheries in Europe, is a legacy those of us who fish the Foyle would wish to leave to our grandchildren.

The Duke of Abercorn

Arthur Stuart on the Duke of Abercorn´s water

MOY

Hᴏᴡ ᴘʟᴇᴀsᴀɴᴛ ɪs ᴛʜᴇ ᴄᴏᴜɴᴛʀʏsɪᴅᴇ of County Mayo in late spring and early summer. The quiet country lanes and stone-walled fields leading to the River Moy sparkle in the bright sun light. The Ox Mountains, where the River Moy rises, are as rugged, beautiful and unspoilt a part of Ireland as one could wish to come across. It is a place where time passes gently and life's pace is taken much more slowly.

Despite its beautiful surroundings, the Moy is not one of the fastest or prettiest salmon rivers in the world. It's lower reaches meander through a large flood plain and it has suffered from a misguided drainage scheme. And the Moy has never been a producer of huge salmon. It's salmon and grilse are, however, magnificent in proportion - short, deep, solid fish that are very pleasing to the eye. And they fight accordingly.

The Moy was renowned for its productivity, for its sheer numbers of salmon. It was an exceptionally prolific grilse river with substantial spring and autumn salmon runs. Every pool and run had fresh leaping fish. The mild Irish climate helped produce vast shoals of silver smolts which migrated downriver every spring. We watched and knew that many would return as adults one or two years later. It was a river where the specific colour of a dyed hackle on an Irish shrimp fly warranted more importance than almost anything else on any particular day. The Moy was also renowned for its consistency, with Loughs Conn and Cullin providing water flow even after many weeks without rainfall.

The Moy is also a river of sand martins, my favourite bird. I marvel at their remarkable precision and control in flight. They love to play above the river, flying close to the surface into the wind and suddenly turning back downwind with spectacular aerobatics. The sand martins and the first salmon of the year both arrived in early spring. Watching the airborne antics of the sand martins, one would regularly see salmon leaping below, white spray from their splashes blown back in the wind.

The sand martins still return to the Moy as usual. You may still watch them gleefully darting and gliding above the river surface. But the once common sight of spring salmon leaping in the background is now rare. When I was learning the skills of fly fishing on the Moy, there could not have been a better place. Fish were abundant and there was easy access to the river. Sadly, and indeed so very needlessly, after years of drift netting this is no longer so.

Along the Coolcronan Fishery

Ridge Pool Stone

The vast numbers of fish that made it so easy to learn simply are not there any more to teach the aspiring fly fisher. It is a great and tragic loss.

But down on the tidal water, where the Moy runs through the center of Ballina Town, the few grilse that somehow avoided the nets still congregate. The famous Ridge Pool and Cathedral Beat still hold fish, especially in low water. Angling tourists can still be seen fly fishing there throughout the summer. This provides an attraction to visitors and adds a special quality to Ballina Town. Spectators watch salmon and grilse leap, and wager on whether a hooked fish will be landed. Those of us who remember the Moy in its prime know that this fishing is a mere remnant of what used to be, and fervently hope one day will be restored. It could happen, if only the salmon were as free as the sand martins to return to their beloved River Moy.

There is renewed hope. The recent decision of the Irish Government, long overdue, to ban the drift nets on Ireland´s West Coast could help restore the salmon runs in this once great river. We will wait and pray.

Robert Gillespie

The famous Ridge Pool in Ballina

ENGLAND AND WALES

Ian Cook and Ben Simpson at Upexe Mill

DART

AFTER RAIN, OFTEN PLENTIFUL on Dartmoor, the bogs and peaty places of the high moor are pregnant with water. Slowly at first, then swiftly, the marshes give watery birth to streamlets: Wallabrook, Blackabrook, Cherrybrook, 0-brook and others without names. You can step across these runnels at their origins, but by the time they have run a mile or so over impermeable granite they burst, a generous peat-stained flow, into the East and West Dart Rivers. Below the narrow stone bridge at Badger's Holt, East and West unite to form the main Dart River.

Soon after that watery bulge is born and rolling down the valley I am beside the river, rod in hand with floating fly line, 12 pound nylon and an orange bucktail fly to cast upon the developing spate. The Dart has many rocks, boulders and gullies with sharp granite edges. The salmon know this and will cut an 8 pound leader on a snag.

The salmon fishing hours of a spate are few for this fast flowing, clear-water river descends 1500 ft over 20 miles as the cormorant flies, soon finding its way to Totnes and the sea. The course is longer if you add twists, turns and loops but, even so, the water bulge quickly passes down the valley. Thus, you must be on the river bank as the rainstorm passes to catch the rise and fall.

The high altitude top stretches of the Dart are not for ancient anglers with brittle bones for it runs down a steep-sided valley where the banks and bed are pitted with many holes. The river may be viewed from above as it winds, black and snakelike, below the Two Bridges/Dartmeet Road and, more closely as it grows, from one of the single carriage granite bridges in the woods of The Chase at Holne. The fields here are changed from the heather moors to old red sandstone which colours the water in a spate but only for a day before the moorland flow washes the river clean.

The few miles from Buckfast to Totnes are paradise for the mature unathletic angler. There, small wild daffodils nod their yellow heads on grassy banks in spring, and woodpeckers wing in looping flight from rotten stump to hollow rotting tree.

Middle River

The final fishing is in the tidal pool below the Totnes weir and salmon ladder. There, the first sea trout arrive in March and, later in the season in recent years, salmon pause in the pool for rain in the hills to increase the flow to assist their upstream passage to the spawning beds of the high moor.

Fish too the dark hours and settled flows of dry weeks when the Dart yields sea trout to the Silver Stoat and otters take their share. Go then, wade stealthily and, like a burglar in the twilight, steal a salmon or a sea trout, those silver seabourne fish, from this most beautiful river.

Charles Bingham

New Bridge near Ashburton

DEE

FROM THE DAWN OF TIME until the Industrial Revolution the River Dee (Afon Dyfrdwy) was a wild and untamed river flowing unhindered from its headwater Llyn Tegid (Bala Lake) which in turn is fed by a multitude of streams flowing out of the Cambrian Mountains. One of these streams is the Dyfrdwy, the infant River Dee.

Over the centuries it witnessed the arrival of the Roman legions, the rise and fall of Castle Dinias Bran ("Crow Castle"), where the Holy Grail is reputed to be buried, and the establishment and subsequent ruin of the magnificent Valle Crucis Abbey.

The earliest records for the river begin with the formation of the first River Board in 1886 and show that there were then 127 netsmen working the river and, whilst there is no record of the number of salmon running the river, it must have been substantial. The Dee is now the most regulated river in the UK, but remains an important salmon river. A scheme to buy out the remaining 20 nets is now under way and once they are removed, the improved escapement into the river will greatly increase the number of fish available to spawn and multiply.

The river is now tamed by the hand of man and is harnessed to provide water for industrial, agricultural and domestic needs. The Dee flows out of Llyn Tegid controlled by sluices which enable water to be stored in times of excess and released in times of drought. The Dee remains a beautiful river where Atlantic salmon return to its cool headwaters to spawn just as they did in centuries past.

The Dee is a river of contrasts: white water runs, long placid glides and rocky pools where the water bubbles through outcrops and over boulders. There are wonderful runs where the fisherman's fly will work without any need to mend the line until the fly reaches the dangle. All this is against the backdrop of hill and valley. At the village of Carrog, with its picturesque 17th Century bridge, the river runs so adjacent to the village houses that those who are lucky enough to have a riverside garden can fish standing in it.

The salmon is not alone in these beautiful waters; it shares this habitat with two other fish that thrive in the pure fast running water and that are much prized by the fly fisherman: the brown trout and the grayling.

Alan Sanders at The Wall Pool

The Dee can be a great river in its moment. In October 2005 Gordon Wigginton paid a memorable visit. On his second cast of the day his Ally's Shrimp fly was taken with gusto and after a very exciting fight in fast water he landed a 13 pound bar of silver. His luck was not to stop there. In the next pool, a little further down stream, his first cast produced an equally beautiful eight pound hen fish that was quickly returned, to be followed almost immediately by another take by a fish that did not "stick", then a fine two pound sea trout and finally another beautiful fresh salmon. These fish were also returned. Two hours and 40 minutes of pure magic!

The early Britons called the river "Deova" – "The Goddess" or "Holy River". To the fish, insects, birds and other creatures supported by its pure and precious waters, it unquestionably still is.

Alan Sanders and Gordon Wigginton

Valle Crucis Abbey

Above Carrog Bridge

EXE

THE RIVER EXE RISES ON THE HIGH moorland in southwest England known as Exmoor, home of England's largest wild animal, the red deer, which roams the sweeping heather-clad hills.

Fed by the warm, moist westerly winds from the Atlantic Ocean, the moor acts like a giant sponge receiving the water in downpours and slowly releasing it over the drier parts of the year. The late Poet Laureate Ted Hughes described this cycle as "a stone age hand cupped and brimming lifted an offering". From this source spring the headwaters of the Exe, known as "the Chains". Descending south, the little Exe is joined by its main tributary, the Barle, before passing out of the county of Somerset into Devon. There it is fed by other smaller rivers – the Lowman, Culm and Creedy – and passes through the center of Exeter, an ancient city the Romans called Isca, before pouring its "offering" into the English Channel at Exmouth.

The early inhabitants harnessed the flowing waters of the Exe for power to drive their mills and harvested the abundant salmon runs as a convenient food source. Today water consumption for a burgeoning population takes precedence, but still the salmon return.

Poet's Pool

Weir Pool at Weircliff

123

Some 40 years ago, spring salmon would make their way to the junction of the Barle and Exe by April. Nowadays the bulk of the run arrives in the summer and early autumn. In the old days traditional flies like the Blue Charm and Silver Charm were favored, with slowly spun Golden Sprats or Devon Minnows popular on the lower reaches. Today fishermen are more likely to use a Stoats Tail or Ally Shrimp fly or, as one old-timer quipped, "anything with a bit of silver, black or orange".

Fishing a sunk fly through the long runs and glides, like a miniature submarine gliding through the green-gray water, one waits expectantly for the line to become tight and for one of the Exe's elongated, almost eel-like salmon to slice through the water with your fly. Trains at Bickleigh, where the tracks run close by the river, have been known to make unscheduled stops so the passengers can witness this spectacle.

Down through the centuries men and women have fallen in love with this river, but none have described the pleasure they have experienced on the Exe more eloquently than Ted Hughes who lived in Devon and spent many days fishing the Exe. He described salmon as "sensitive glands in the vast disheveled body of nature, as individual meteorological stations responding to rain, storm and wind". He believed fishing for salmon heightened one's depth of awareness and consciousness.

Do we not all believe the same?

Ian Cook

Ben Simpson on Upexe Mill water

Exe Valley from Bickleigh

Ian Cook walking past Hayman´s Lie

Page 121: View from Weircliff House

TYNE

THE RIVER TYNE is the poster child of the effectiveness of determined conservation efforts on Atlantic salmon runs. There was great abundance and the perfect environment for salmon pre the Industrial Revolution. Then high local human population density and "progress" polluted the river and interfered with the salmon's freedom to reach the headwaters. Salmon runs deteriorated to almost nothing only 50 years ago. Luckily, a highly motivated and successful conservation effort evolved. Much of the historic abundance has now been restored.

The restoration has been three-legged. Firstly, the Environment Agency and others instituted efforts which successfully reduced pollution in the river. This job is not complete. Prolonged periods of low water in summer and the associated low oxygen levels can still lead to salmon mortality in the upper estuary around Wylam.

Secondly, the efforts of Peter Gray at the Kielder Hatchery produced the raw material essential to recovery. The stock was down to such low levels that brood stock had to be sourced from other rivers. In spite of their varied parentage, the fish have evolved into the traditional Tyne shape (short, deep and big!). This leads me to believe that salmon evolve to suit a river and genetic integrity is less important to river restoration than some would have us believe.

Thirdly, the buy out of the North East drift nets in 2003 led by Orri Vigfússon and the NASF reduced the number of licensed netsmen to 16 from 142 and had an immediate positive effect on rod catches. It will be exciting to see how that uplift is multiplied as the offspring of those spared from the nets return as adults in future years!

The recorded rod catch has been in excess of 4000 salmon in recent years (from 0 in the 1950's). This makes the Tyne the most productive salmon river in England. The restoration has been greatly helped by the catch-and-release culture that, while mandatory up to June 16th, is increasingly becoming the voluntary norm among Tyne fishers. The recent establishment of the Tyne Rivers Trust should ensure a bright future.

I have talked of the Tyne, but it is really made up of two very different rivers in the upper reaches. The South Tyne is a clear river which drains the northern tip of the Pennines. It is highly sensitive to rainfall and fishes best

Roman Bridge at Chollerford, North Tyne

after a spate. The North Tyne is dominated by Kielder Water near its source. It is a peaty tinged river and its levels are artificially controlled by releases from this reservoir. This is a mixed blessing, for while it enables spates to be created in dry periods in summer and fish to run, some say the coldness of the released water puts the fish off the take.

The two rivers join at Watersmeet, just above Hexham. It is hard to believe that two relatively small rivers can spawn such a great one when looking over Hexham Bridge after rain. You never have to look for long before Salmo the Leaper lives up to his name! The river takes on the peaty characteristic of her northern parent. She offers some great fly water on her sinuous course to the sea at Newcastle-upon-Tyne.

The peaty tinge of the main Tyne means that any fly is fine so long as it is orange! My favourites are Ally's Shrimp and Cascade patterns tied on quite small (12 and 14) hooks. The added bonus of small flies is that you often catch lovely sea trout on them in the middle of the day. The best runs of salmon seem to be in autumn and they often run big with 20 pounders quite commonplace and the magical 30 pound barrier broken several times each year. What better way to celebrate a conservation success story than to spend a September day trying for the new monsters of the Tyne!

Jeremy Herrmann

Good evening for angling

WYE AND USK

WALES IS BLESSED BY THE BREATHTAKING beauty of the Usk and Wye Rivers as they meander from the central uplands to empty into the Severn Estuary only 20 miles apart. Together they drain an area of some 2300 sq. miles of south and eastern Wales. From their headwaters in the hills they flow through the lush agricultural lands of Hereford and Monmouthshire to the sea, providing every conceivable shape and size of pool, riffle and flat along the way. Enchanting scenes with strong links to Britain's Roman past grace their banks. Both rivers, however, have had a chequered history in respect of salmon runs.

The Wye rod catch was reduced to just a few hundred fish by the end of the 20th Century. The first ever buy out of nets brought a well documented recovery. Between 1920 and 1980, the Wye was the preeminent spring salmon river of England and Wales, prized for its early running fish which averaged over 20 pounds. The largest was a leviathan of 59 ½ pounds caught in 1929. Today the Wye is again recovering from the effects of barriers to migration, water quality problems and loss of juvenile habitat.

The 40 pound plus fish that were once prevalent in the Wye may be long gone, but annually this, the best known salmon river in England and Wales, surrenders fish of over 30 pounds, some even taken in the picturesque "gutters" of the upper river. The Wye slows down in its middle reaches to beautiful glides, deep pools and fast runs that are overlooked by rows of stately trees that stand like sentries on duty guarding these precious jewels.

Rod catches on the Usk reached their nadir in the early 1990's, brought on by a combination of poor estuarial water quality and legal and illegal netting. Less than 200 fish were caught. At present the Usk is the most productive river in Wales and there are plans to further improve the salmon runs by constructing fish passes around obstructions and juvenile habitat restoration. The Usk is similar to the Wye in many respects, but is more of a "late" river. It has always had a spring run, but over the years this has given way to more summer and autumn fish.

Both rivers suffered extensively from the pollution caused by the Industrial Revolution and more recently from changes in land use. Sheep grazing and commercial forestry in their upper catchment areas and extensive agricultural activities and the accompanying demands for water abstraction in their middle and lower reaches have contributed to the problems. But

Bridge Pool, Wye

Fishing hut on Usk

Sheep along the Usk

the splendour of these rivers defies these ravages. They continue to offer anglers the challenge and opportunity to test their skills against some of the biggest salmon that the UK can offer and in a setting of unequaled beauty and charm.

And the future looks bright. In 2000 NASF, together with the Wye and Usk Foundation and landowners and fishermen of both rivers, signed an agreement to end drift netting and "putcher" fishing in the Severn estuary (banks of traps that catch salmon on the rise and fall of the highest tides in the world) over several years. This has already resulted in a huge boost in the summer salmon fishing, with beats in the lower sections of the rivers now fishing as well as ever. When all estuary exploitation ceases, these wonderful rivers are well placed to rise again in the annals of the world class salmon fisheries.

Gareth Edwards

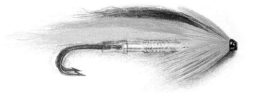

Scene on Wye

Page 133: Little waterfall on Usk

SCOTLAND

Naver

Helmsdale

Deveron

Aberdeen

Spey

Dee

North Esk

South Esk

Tay

Glasgow

Edinburgh

Tweed

Scott´s View, River Tweed

DEE

HOME TO SCOTLAND'S GREATEST spring run of Atlantic salmon, the sublime River Dee flows 130 km from the heart of the Cairngorm Mountains to its mouth in the city of Aberdeen. Some of the oldest rocks in the world are found in the north-east of Scotland. The varied geology of the area, in terms of time and rock types, is almost as old in geological time scales. Rising at the Wells of Dee – a series of mountain pools located above 1200 metres on the upper slopes of Braeriach – the Dee flows clear and fast, over hard worn granite bedrock before tumbling over the precipitous Linn of Dee and through the magnificent scenery of Royal Deeside.

In 1847 Queen Victoria's doctor reported that her son, while recuperating from illness on Deeside, had benefited greatly from a period of particularly fine weather. Climate reports called for by Prince Albert confirmed that the area was drier than parts of the west. In 1848 the Royal couple leased Balmoral and fell in love with Deeside – the young Queen wrote "All seemed to breathe freedom and peace, and to make one forget the world and all its sad turmoils". The rest is history, and each summer the Royal Family return to Balmoral to enjoy all the pleasures their revered ancestor found here.

Balmoral Castle

Polvier Pool, Birkhall Beat

Victorian anglers enjoyed some of the finest fishing in the Dee´s history – and their modernising approach to tackle design is reflected in today´s equipment. Victorian tackle gave rise to many of the rods and reels we know today.

No longer were salmon played on a "tight line" or one tied to the rod tip. Loose lines now ran through rod rings. It was on the Dee that A.H.E. Wood perfected his world-famous method of greased line fishing.

The classic fly fishing River Dee is divided into three parts – upper, middle and lower. Spring salmon arrive early here – by opening day (1st February) they are well distributed through the lower reaches, at least as far as Banchory – even if the winter is cold. Mild winters can mean good fishing much farther upstream – at least as far as Aboyne in March. By the end of April, significant numbers of springers should be present in the upper reaches – May and June are prime months here. In addition to the spring salmon run, the river also provides excellent summer fishing for salmon, grilse and sea trout.

Since 1995 a catch-and-release policy has allowed tens of thousands of fish to be released back to the river to continue upstream to their spawning grounds. All salmon and sea trout netting within the river and along the coast of the Dee fishery district has been stopped – conservation measures entirely in tune with the catchment area's recognised value in terms of nature conservation – it is a designated Special Area of Conservation.

For decades fly fishermen have extolled the clarity of this sparkling river – widely regarded as one of the least contaminated of the country's larger rivers. Anyone passionate about fly fishing will, inevitably, fall in love with the Dee and Deeside – its mountains, wildlife and stunning scenery combine to make this a truly irresistible piscatorial experience.

As a boy, I was told that golf was Scotland's passion – but fishing was its religion! Continuing the analogy, I have to confess that, even now, I never cease to revel in "worshipping" on Deeside.

Stewart Spence

Fish hut, Grey Mare Pool

Cottage Pool

Grey Mare Pool

DEVERON

THE DEVERON HAS BEEN dubbed the "hidden gem" of Scottish salmon rivers, a secret jealously guarded by those who fish it. But to a wider public it is best known for producing Britain's largest fly-caught salmon.

The Deveron rises in the wild Cabrach plateau, a land of grouse and calling curlew high in the West Aberdeenshire foothills of the Grampian Mountains. It starts life as a peaty burn, but near Huntly the tumbling pace slackens. Here the main stream is swelled by the Bogie, a once-renowned sea trout river ruined by forestry but ripe for revival. Downstream the Isla joins the system at Rothiemay.

Now the growing stream meanders east to the market town of Turriff and finally north to its mouth at Banff on the Moray Firth, 60 miles from the source.

After the more famous Spey, Tay, Tweed and Dee, the Deveron is Scotland's fifth salmon river. Its charm lies in the unspoilt and even unpretentious country through which it flows. This is a soft landscape of fertile farm and woodland, steep sunny banks, lost roads and glimpsed views; a land of few modern interruptions.

Throughout its length run follows glide but it is often in the slower-moving sections that the angler will experience the long slow pull of a taking salmon. Fish up to 20 or 30 pounds may be caught at any time between February and October, but especially in the late summer and autumn. Early in the year the upper beats tend to be the most successful. Cascades, Munro Killers and Ally Shrimps are proven flies.

The brown trout fishing in April and May is renowned and in 2005 a wild ten pounder was caught on the Isla. June and July see the arrival of sea trout, still one of the most exciting fish to catch in late dusk with bats on the wing, the splash of a fish in the gloaming and a dram waiting in the fishing hut. The sea trout may have declined in recent years, but pressure to halt the industrial fishing for sand eels, a primary food source, may help restore stocks. These Deveron sea trout can weigh in at five pounds. The grilse too will start running around July.

But it is for "The Morison Fish" that the Deveron is better known. In October 1924 Mrs. "Tiny" Morison of Mountblairy, Turriff landed a 61 pound fish

Looking down on Log Pool, Upper Netherdale

that was only a whisker short of the more famous 64 pound Tay fish caught on live bait. Mrs. Morison hooked the cock fish on a 1 1/4-inch long Brown Wing Killer fly. It took just half an hour to land. It was so big that Sim, the ghillie, could not haul it up the bank and Mrs. Morison had to go down, seize it by the gills and help drag it from the water's edge. After a plaster cast had been taken the fish was "kippered" (smoked) and chunks handed out to estate staff.

In spite of the chance of big fish, the Deveron is seldom a threatening river. It is big enough to be a challenge, but neither intimidating nor monotonous. A generally shingly bottom makes wading uncomplicated. Thigh waders and an 11 foot rod will usually be enough to cover water that can rise or fall significantly within 24 hours. Today the Deveron, Bogie and Isla Charitable Trust is restoring habitat, removing obstacles and re-stocking. Twenty two miles of the system have been reopened for spawning.

The Deveron may be less imposing and less well known than some of its grander neighbours. But that, for those that know it, is its very charm and attraction.

Alastair Robertson

Fishing hut at Glennie

Page 143: Mayen from Fourman Hill

142

HELMSDALE

Many SCOTTISH FISHERS, offered a choice of any river in which to cast a fly for a salmon, would take the Helmsdale. If it lacks the majesty of Tweed or the prettiness of the neighbouring Naver, it possesses an intimacy and variety which charm every rod who knows it. Only 20 miles long, it descends the Strath of Kildonan to the east coast of Sutherland with a whimsy which provides a wonderful range of fishing on six rotating beats. There are twisting flats and steep falls, peaty banks and slow, wide expanses with sandy shores. The swift eddies through the midst of many pools look every fisherman's idea of places that should hold fish – and usually do.

The descent to the sea from the hill lochs where the river rises is only a matter of 400 feet, but in places it drops with exciting steepness, a fine holding pool beneath each craggy fall. Although salmon respond to rain as sensitively on the Helmsdale as on any other river, the headwater dam makes it possible to boost flow in the summer months, and makes every low-water fisher grateful.

It is a decade and more since the Helmsdale yielded the big July grilse runs of former times, but it is a poor week when there are not fish in the river. Every rod knows the special thrill of fishing the adjoining Whinnie and Marrel pools at the bottom of Beat One, where the latest fish to come in with the tide are found, and even duffers often triumph.

An angling enthusiast wrote almost a century ago: "There is perhaps no river in Scotland where good days are more frequent than the Helmsdale". Even now, when catch numbers are down and the cost of renting a two-rod beat is as high as that for any fishing in Britain, this remains true.

There are few greater joys than to fish one of the upper beats in July with a single-handed rod, flicking a Temple Dog or Willie Gunn into the intimate corners each pool can boast; or to try a long line across the lower reaches, knowing that any day it could be your turn to catch one of the handful of seriously big fish which the Helmsdale yields every season. Here is a river that boasts some of the wildest vistas and best catches in northern Scotland. If a man who covets your wife owns a beat on the Helmsdale, don't hesitate.

Max Hastings

The Pot (low water)

NAVER

Bᴜᴢᴢᴀʀᴅs ᴄɪʀᴄʟɪɴɢ ʜɪɢʜ in the sky with the sun on their backs. An osprey hovering, searching for his lunch. Deer grazing on the hillside. A bright silver salmon leaping in the pool in front of you. Is this a dream? No. This is the River Naver.

The Naver in Sutherland flows for approximately 17 miles from the outlet of Loch Naver to the sea, entering at Torrisdale Bay in the small town of Bettyhill on the northernmost coast of mainland Scotland. The scenery as the river tumbles and falls on it journey to the sea is wild moors, forests and farmland, as fresh and stunning as the morning sunrise.

A more beautiful 17 miles of river would be hard to find.

Throughout its length the Naver has an excellent variety of fishing. There are no fewer than 109 pools, all untouched by human hand. There are no obstructions from the sea to the Loch. The fish are spread through the pools and into the Loch from the earliest spring day. These pools vary in character from long glides to short bubbling streams and from deep pools to shallow runs. There are high water pools as well as a number of excellent pools for summer fishing. The Naver has fishing for all conditions.

The Naver is not a large, powerful river like the better known Scottish rivers to the south. And, although a fish of 30 pounds was caught in the Angling Club water near the mouth of the river several years ago and 20 pounders are taken every year, it is not famous for big fish. It is instead a smaller, more

Doctors Pool

Crack Pool (upper river)

intimate river. Those who love big rivers, deep wading and endless casts may not fully appreciate the Naver, or understand how best to lure its prolific stocks of salmon. It is not a water that intimidates or physically challenges the angler. Rather it offers fishing in an idyllic and contemplative setting where each cast has to be thought out with care.

The river itself, as well as the tributaries (the main one being the Mallart which is an excellent little river in its own right), contains an excellent bed of clean spawning gravel which hosts a healthy population of juvenile fish and fresh water mussels. There is no pollution, and the gravel on the river bed is as clean as can be. Loch Naver is a natural filter that leaves the river running gin clear in every condition except flood. Is it any wonder that the returning adults do not resist their instinctive drive to return to their point of origin to lay their eggs when it involves such a beautiful journey to such unspoiled surroundings?

In the past, the salmon in the Naver were in decline, as was the case with most other salmon rivers in Scotland. Over the last four or five years, however, salmon runs have been showing a steady increase, which may be due to the restocking program over the last 13 years, as well as a catch-and-release policy that the Naver Fishery Board has recently put in place. This seems to be working well, with over 50-60% of all fish caught now being released to continue their epic journey upstream. The work and effort of all connected with the Board has been invaluable to the restoration of the fish stocks in the Naver.

Our dream is to return to those red letter days when there was an abundance of fish in every pool on the river.

Archie Baillie

Wall at Crack Pool

Old smokehouse

Naver entering the North Sea

NORTH AND SOUTH ESKS

THE ESKS RISE HIGH in the Grampian Mountains before flowing eastwards into the North Sea between the Tay and the Dee. Similar in size, they run at first through the Angus Glens, before tumbling through rocky, tree-lined ravines into the fertile farmland of the coastal plain. The rivers are close neighbours, but quite different geologically and structurally, with the North Esk generally more fertile with a catchment shaped like a chestnut tree, and the South Esk with more acidic water, its system shaped like a poplar tree, and with its unique tidal lake, Montrose Basin.

Fishing hut, Finovan Castle Water, South Esk

Both rivers offer salmon, grilse and sea trout fishing of exceptional quality. In the low river levels of high summer, when sea trout shoals gather in the larger pools, and grilse filter upstream under cover of darkness, a stealthy approach is needed by the angler to have any chance of catching these wary fish. With the heavier flows of spring and autumn, salmon run strongly into the upper reaches, providing an excellent show of fish in all the main pools.

The North Esk is renowned for its prolific runs of salmon and grilse. The river flows out of Loch Lee in Glen Esk, and its main tributary, the West

The Ladies' Walk, Cortachy, South Esk

151

Water, is a crystal clear stream, with a good reputation for grilse and sea trout. The main stem of the North Esk, from the confluence with the West Water to the sea, is in the top rank of Scottish salmon rivers. Autumn catches of salmon are better than ever, and spring salmon and summer grilse fishing are improving each year. Beats below Morphie Dyke on the lower river are famous for their spring salmon.

The South Esk flows from its source on the Balmoral Estate, with clear water of exceptional quality, through the spectacular countryside of Glen Clova. Its main tributary, the Prosen, is itself a fine upland salmon river, and runs into the South Esk at Cortachy. From there the river flows some 25 miles to the sea. It is a good spring and autumn salmon river, with the added reputation of being Scotland's best sea trout river. The exciting sport of night fishing for these elusive and mysterious fish is part of the local culture. As a Europe-designated conservation river, the South Esk benefits from a range of special measures to improve habitat and enhance the natural environment.

The potential of both Esks is now being realised, as better management, habitat improvements and reduction of coastal netting take effect. In the next few years these two fertile and prolific rivers are likely to show increased runs of fish, and to confirm their place as two of Scotland's prime angling destinations. These are rivers with a growing reputation, and a great future ahead of them.

Tony Andrews

Canterland Beat, North Esk

Craigo Stream, Finavon, South Esk

Couperee, Orton

SPEY

Talehun, above Stránn Pool

Kincardine and Kinchurdy

THE SPEY TAKES NO PRISONERS. I know it as a fearsome water, heavy, serious, gurgling, even menacing. When you advance into its turbulent torrent your nerves are steeled. The water is clear, with a slight tinge the colour of the whisky produced at the 30 some distilleries along its banks. This is no bottom-of-the-garden stream. Your legs feel the push of the fastest flowing major river in Britain. The river bed is boulders. You are here to be tested.

The Spey originates over 1000 feet above sea level in the Monadhliath Mountains and flows north-east for almost 100 miles until it meets the Moray Firth at Spey Bay. Apart from its middle reaches, where it meanders through the alluvial plane of Strathspey, the gradient is steep, producing the fast current. The heavily wooded banks along parts of the Spey make the conventional overhead cast impossible. The Spey cast was devised to overcome these limitations.

I do not fish the Spey regularly. But those days on the river are etched well on my memory. I recall this particular atmosphere. Down through the wooded farm land of the middle beats the angler is secluded away from passing spectators. Cattle graze the banks. Ducks climb quacking into the air from coverts of willow and alder. There is a tangle of broken branches to remind you that this is a river of mighty spates riding fast flows. High heather moors form the skyline. Behind, the Central Grampians, the main rock massif of the British Isles, huddle together in brooding assembly.

Anglers earn a fish on the Spey. Things do not happen unless you make them. No one catches a Spey salmon without decent effort. You win a fish from the stream; there is no let-up of tension until it is truly beached. Spey salmon know they are in Scotland's proudest river.

Apart from its renowned salmon, the Spey is one of Scotland's best sea trout rivers and has a resident population of fine brown trout. In summer darkness the sea trout start splashing. You hear their nervy flipping. If you hook one, it has the fine electric energy of a fish in its own precinct. With bats flitting by the trees and through the shadows you get again that feeling of power the Spey generates without effort.

To take up the challenge of this river requires a masterfulness not called upon in milder streams. Brace yourselves!

Michael Wigan

Auldearg, Brae Water

TAY

THE TAY IS BRITAIN'S LARGEST RIVER, drawing its waters from the misty highland glens in the west 100 miles across country through Loch Tay to the arable straths in the east where it enters the Firth of Tay at Perth. It drains 3000 sq. miles of Scotland en route. Rivers such as the Dochart, Lyon, Tummel, Garry, Tilt, Isla, Ericht, Ardle, Shee, Braan, Almond and Earn all contribute their own indigenous salmon runs toward the Tay's prolific rod fishery. Large lochs and hydroelectric dams in the headwaters generally help maintain good flow levels throughout the year, and thus the river could well be described as drought resistant.

Bridge at Aberfeldy

The cyclical nature of salmon runs has become increasingly apparent with warmer weather encouraging later runs and spawning. The fishing season currently runs from January 15 until October 15 with March-May and July-October the best times. The wintry start of the season is commemorated each year by the ceremonial pouring of a quaich of whisky over the bow of the first boat to head out at Kenmore to a background skirl of bagpipes. The historic runs of three-sea-winter fish have never recovered from high seas netting and the UDN disease than ravaged the river decades ago, but the Tay remains famous as a big fish river. The British record was caught on the Tay on 7 October 1922, by young Miss Georgina Ballantine. She had already caught fish of 17 and 25 pounds that morning. At the end of the day her last

Upper Carse Pool

cast produced a violent take and, after a two hour struggle, her father gaffed the 64 pound monster. An 84 pound fish was reported to have been taken in a net in 1869. Those days are long gone, but my best fish of over 40 pounds shows that respectable fish still inhabit the Tay.

Fly fishing is the preferred and most popular fishing method, although spin fishing is often employed in high water. Fishermen lucky enough to be tended by that fount of wit and knowledge, the Tay Ghillie, often fish using the "harling" technique from a traditional Tay boat or coble. Not a particularly skillful way to fish perhaps, but quite effective, and especially well suited for the less able. The Tay's tributaries and upper reaches provide lovely stream fishing in classic Scottish surroundings and can all be fished with a single-handed fly rod, but lower down the main stream's imposing width requires sterner tackle. 17 and 18 foot double-handled rods are quite common. The river has spawned such famous fly patterns as the Dunkeld, Green Highlander and Hairy Mary.

Estuarine netting was historically the scourge of the Tay with annual catches exceeding 40,000 salmon and grilse as recently as the 1980's. Fortunately wisdom prevailed and a buy out was completed in 1997. The Tay Board, guided by the pragmatic Dr. David Summers, has banned fishing with shrimp and prawn, encouraged catch-and-release and pursued an extensive hatchery and stocking program. These encouraging developments, combined with NASF's wonderful work to limit high seas netting in the salmon's winter feeding grounds and North Sea, makes for an optimistic future for the Tay.

Michael C. Smith

Corner Pool

Fishing hut at Corner Pool

TWEED

TWEED (traditionally referred to without the definite article), along with the Dee, Spey and Tay, is considered one of the four great salmon rivers of Britain. She provides the border between Scotland and England for much of her course. Her bridges are corridors along which armies flowed; sometimes south, more often north. The castles and keeps which line her banks speak of a long and bloody history. On the banks of Tweed Scotland's most renown writer and poet, Sir Walter Scott, built his home, Abbotsford House, and wrote many of his famous works.

Tweed does not tumble down steep forested gradients, nor cut a swath through dramatic highland mountain scenery. There are no waterfalls or impressive rapids, and her water – even in the upper reaches – is never truly crystal clear. Yet, she has the ability to capture a fisher's heart. More words have been written about "bonnie Tweed" than any other salmon river. She has inspired much of angling's greatest literature. One only has to open classics like William Scrope's *Days and Nights of Salmon Fishing* (1843) or John Younger's *River Angling for Salmon and Trout* (1840) to step back in time to a world of vast catches and monsters fought and lost. Flies such as the world famous Greenwell's Glory, Garry Dog, Thunder & Lighting, Silver Doctor, Jock Scott and more recent patterns like the Junction Shrimp were fashioned on her banks.

Tweed also has the ability to break a fisher's heart. The valley through which she runs, the Merse, is fertile with rich red soil and a lowland character. Changes in the hydrology of this valley over the years, made in the interest of "drainage improvement", have substantially increased ground water run-off into the river. Less rain water now soaks into the ground to be naturally filtered before slowly seeping into the river. Today's rapid run off gives rise to Tweed's frequent coloured floods. Gone are the days when the Tweed was described as "running high and clear for weeks on end". The combination of the plentiful rains that characterize the weather patterns of the British Isles and the time it now takes the river to clear (perceived wisdom is that fishing is not really worthwhile till the second day after a flood) results in a high percentage of fishing days being lost each season.

If, however, you like to gamble with the weather gods and do not mind risking "feast or famine", the rewards can be great. When "in good order", Tweed can match the best fishing Russia has to offer. Individual catches of over ten fish a day are not uncommon and, although the average weight

Above Norham Bridge

of the autumn run has declined in recent years, 20 pound plus fish are still caught regularly. Indeed, a magnificent 41 pound fish was caught in a net at the mouth of the river last autumn, and a veritable monster was subsequently photographed in one of the upstream fish counters.

The season starts at the beginning of February and runs all the way through November. Barely a generation ago Tweed was regarded as a spring river. While salmon are still reported to run in throughout the year, Tweed is now renown as a "back-end" river.

The buy out of the North East drift nets (orchestrated by NASF and others in 2002) is having a very positive effect on salmon runs in Tweed, with recorded rod catches in the last three seasons averaging over 14,000 fish – an increase of over 40%. This makes Tweed the most prolific river in Britain. The reduction in commercial netting, the enlightened management of the river's entire catchment area by the Tweed Foundation (a template for river management everywhere) and the changing attitudes of fishermen regarding catch-and-release, all should contribute to a bright future for Tweed.

No article on Tweed would be complete without some mention of the "Tweed Boatman". No one term, "companion", "friend", "guide" or "ghillie", does justice to this unique breed of watermen who will without complaint (well, perhaps "rarely a complaint"!) row all day, often in the teeth of a bitter east wind, skillfully dropping down one of Tweed's famous "dubs" to allow the fisher to thoroughly cover the water. These fine gentlemen provide a connection to Tweed's glorious past and one of the reasons fishing on Tweed should continue to be such a special experience in the future. I salute them all.

Every visit to Tweed is for me a pilgrimage paying homage to the history, tradition and mystery that is Atlantic salmon fishing at its best.

Richard Vainer

Bordermaid Pool

Tweed in autumm

Tweedmill

Page 163: Brendan Lough and Kevin Wright on Cornhill Beat

NORWAY, SWEDEN AND FINLAND

Alta

Tana

Namsen

Stjørdal

● Trondheim

Orkla   *Gaula*

FINLAND

Lærdal

Bergen ●

NORWAY

Oslo ●

● Helsinki

SWEDEN

● Stockholm

Em

Mörrum

Aurland Fjord, Norway

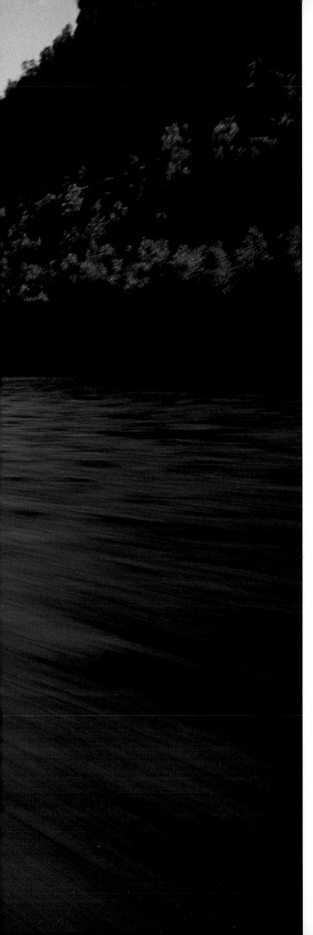

ALTA

The LEGENDARY ALTA RIVER is the best known salmon river in the world and has a long and distinguished sport fishing history over the last 150 years. The Alta's fame and glory stem from the number of big fish the river produces and its beauty and solitude, situated as it is in the land of the midnight sun 300 miles north of the Arctic Circle. These attributes combine to offer a unique and emotional experience to the fortunate few who get the opportunity to fish this marvelous river.

The Alta is a wide river with fast and powerful runs and deep and mysterious holding pools. It is a river of great variety and it would be insane to fish with anything else but fly. The river is surprisingly temperate considering its location in the most northern reaches of Norway. This is because it is generally shallow and not glacier fed. The water is warmer than the sea. The water is also relatively clear, although the dark riverbed reflects a brownish tinge.

About to be released

The fishing season starts in the middle of June when the sun is at its highest point. Fishermen do not venture out until eight in the evening and then fish throughout the night when the sun's rays no longer glare directly down into the long pools, but are absorbed by the surrounding mountains and woods of Europe's deepest canyon. At midnight driftwood is collected, a fire is lit

Parila Pool

167

on the river bank and the fishermen break for coffee made in an iron smoke-blackened kettle and a delicious meal of perhaps sausages and barbecued chicken legs. This is a time for reflection, idle gossip, laughter and rest before the final session when the biggest fish often stir during the early dawn.

The fabled waters of the Alta offer perfect fly water throughout their descent and on any pool one can anticipate the fishing sensation of a lifetime – the slow draw of a 40 or even 50 pounder turning on the fly. But the Alta is so steeped in tradition, atmosphere and legend that only a person lacking a soul would, when casting, be able to concentrate his or her mind entirely on the salmon pool.

The Alta Laksefiskeri Interessentskap ("ALI") are the guardians of the river. Their regulations keep fishing pressure to a minimum, permitting only ten rods throughout 17 miles of water for much of the season. Guards patrol the riverbanks day and night to deter nefarious activities. Catch-and-release has become an accepted and encouraged practice and now most locals and foreigners release a large percentage of the fish they catch. Nets in the river mouth still take too large a percentage of the returning fish in the beginning of the season, especially large fish. But the ALI, under the leadership of its former Chairman, Ivar Leinan, is working on a solution. Fortunately, the river plays such a significant part in the lives of those who live nearby that all wish to see it thrive and prosper.

David Hoare

Beautiful rainbow

Typical Alta Boat at Richardola

GAULA

THE GAULA IS A CAPRICIOUS RIVER, changing with the seasons, weeks, days and even hours. Winding her way down from the old mining town of Røros to the fjord near the medieval capital of Norway, Trondheim, she is in torrential flood one day and low the next.

The Gaula is clear, but not a blue river. The word "Gul" means yellow in Norwegian, and it is thought that the colour of the river after a heavy downpour, like French cognac, might explain its name. The narrow valley is covered by lush green forests on the steep hillsides and that, combined with the golden tint of the water, explains the success of flies in green and yellow, brown and orange. The beautiful Green Highlander is an efficient fly on this river, as are modern Scandinavian tube flies dressed in brown and red or black and gold.

Norwegian Flyfishers Club Home Pool

Salmon runs are strong from early June till late August, a mix of one-, two- and three-sea-winter fish, with even an occasional four-sea-winter fish. Nowadays, this river is one of the few in Norway which can justifiably be described as a big-fish river. Each year, numerous salmon above 25 pound are caught, and in 2005 the 20 largest recorded fish weighted in above 40 pounds! The biggest was a magnificent fish of almost 21 kilograms caught on a small black tube fly. From early June, these huge salmon can be seen attacking a fly in the upper pools of the river, more than 50 miles from the sea.

Manfred Raguse in upper Langøy Pool

171

From an angling perspective, the Gaula has several markedly different sections. The lower part from the sea to the Gaulfoss pool is a mix of huge glides suitable for fly fishing and deep pools more suitable for fishing with spoons and bait. But starting at the Gaulfoss pool, the river is a fly angler's dream! The Gaulfoss pool itself is among the most famous and productive salmon pools in the world, especially early in the season. Upwards, the river changes swiftly between mysterious pools, smooth runs and exciting whitewater rapids. Here, you can fish the same pools that the British pioneers fished in the mid-1800's. Pools such as Frøseth, Kroken and Flaskehølen have attracted more than 15 generations of anglers!

The banks of the Gaula have been a major arena for the development of modern Scandinavian salmon fly fishing. In no other place will you find a more impressive gathering of crafty casters and skilled fish hunters. Armed with state-of-the-art rods, reels and lines, anglers demonstrating the characteristic rhythm of the modern Spey cast can be seen everywhere. At the end of their leaders you will often find a hair-wing fly made of soft foxhair, tied on a one inch tube or size 2- 6 double hook. The Gaula was one of the legendary Lee Wulff's favourite Norwegian rivers, and this explains why the Gaula is one of the few rivers in Norway with a significant dry fly tradition.

The last few years have seen improvements in salmon stocks after the disappointing 1990's. After a protracted fight, the river gained protection from further hydro development in the 1980's. Steps were taken to reduce the toxic runoff from closed down mines which had had a major impact on smolt production in the past. Recently, the river owners entered into a significant agreement with netsmen in the fjord restricting their catch. This agreement was based on NASF's policy of salmon conservation and strongly supported by Orri Vigfússon. The future of this marvellous fishery looks bright.

Øystein Aas

Pasge 173: So many choices

LÆRDAL

THE LÆRDAL AND THE ALTA are probably the two most famous salmon rivers in Norway. And the Lærdal is certainly among the most beautiful. Beginning at its mouth on the Lærdal Fjord, one of the arms of Norway's longest fjord, the Sognefjord, which is approximately half way between Oslo and Bergen on Norway's west coast, the river runs through the stunningly beautiful Lærdal Valley with rocky peaks towering above the river and waterfalls cascading down the steep hillsides. Its waters are extremely clear, with a tinge of blue. The watercourse is intimate, yet big enough to challenge the most expert angler.

Before disaster struck in 1996, the Lærdal was a highly productive salmon river yielding its share of 30+ pound salmon and even the occasional 50 pounder. While it certainly deserved to be classified among the world's most prolific salmon rivers, when compared to certain other Norwegian rivers it may not have had runs of the largest salmon or the highest catches. But with the exception of the Alta, no river in Norway has a reputation to match it. The late Ernest Schwiebert, a great admirer and advocate of the Lærdal, asks in one of his wonderful stories why this was so. He provided the answer himself - the Lærdal's heritage, one that is unrivalled in the salmon world. Kings and queens, politicians, businessmen and celebrities have been regular visitors. If name dropping was a competition among salmon rivers, the Lærdal would win hands down. Norway's King Harald, Denmark's Prince Axel, England's Winston Churchill, polar explorer Fridtjof Nansen and singer, guitarist and composer Eric Clapton are just a few of the notables who have fished here.

The Lærdal is also the home of the Atlantic Salmon Center and the most famous fly tier of Norway, Olaf Olsen. During the 1960's, 1970's and 1980's, his workshop and his guiding business earned an unrivaled reputation. Olaf's father, Andreas, was also a legendary fly tier and invented many of the classical fly patterns that can be seen pictured in fly tying books. His brother Alf also guided, and together this family has become a major part of the river's great heritage. It was also on the Lærdal that Ray Brooks created the Sunray Shadow. This simple tube fly, with an overall length of 6-8 inches, soon replaced the old classics on the Lærdal and the Alta. While not having their grace and colour, the Sunray Shadow is popular with anglers because it seems to attract fish up out of deep pools and hook them better. Today the fly is used on salmon rivers everywhere and is especially popular in Iceland and Russia as well as Norway.

Lower Lysne Pool

Tragically, the once glorious Lærdal was infected by the parasite Gyrodactylus salaris in 1996. This fluke, which kills salmon parr, is not native to Norway, and was spread to Norway unintentionally in the late 1970s from the Baltic Sea. Later, during the first half of the 1980's, the parasite was spread via hatchery fish to great rivers like the Rauma, Driva and Vefsna, though how it came to the Lærdal is still unknown. Until recently, the only cure has been to exterminate the fish completely with the poison rotenone. A brood stock is thereafter used to reestablish the population. Twice the Lærdal was treated with rotenone, but both times the parasite somehow survived. In the last few years a new method of treatment has been discovered based on aluminum salts. This treatment does not kill the fish, just the parasite. An intense program has been running on the river during 2005 and 2006, and now everyone is saying a small prayer each night. So far, so good!

Today anglers alongside the picturesque pools Hunderi, Bø and Bjørkum are still catching the odd salmon entering the river, but most of the catch is made up of sea trout which still flourish in the river because this species is not killed by the parasite. All hope and pray for a return of the great salmon runs.

Øystein Aas and Olav Wendelbo

Svend Brooks with Lærdal salmon

Sunray Shadows on Bogdan Reels

Lower Blaaflat Pool

NAMSEN

I HAVE HAD A LONG AND EMOTIONAL relationship with another lady most of my life. A magnificent lady. Powerful and strong. I call her simply "the Queen", as do most others who know her well. My wife included. This queen is the Namsen, the Queen among salmon rivers. She is one of the most beautiful rivers in Norway, running powerfully down the magical Namdal Valley to her mouth on the Namsenfjord. She is also one of Norway's top salmon rivers in terms of catch and size of fish.

My first meeting with the Queen was as a young boy. Accompanied by my father and one of his fishing companions, we headed for the Fiskumfoss, a waterfall below which are some of the best salmon pools on the river. I was thrilled, and not a little scared, at the prospect. It wasn't that fishing was a new activity for me. I was already an experienced angler, having caught some respectable brown trout. But fishing for salmon! And in some of the best salmon pools on the mighty Namsen. This was fishing at an entirely different level. It had a startling effect on a young boy's mind.

I do not recall if we caught any salmon that day long ago. Somehow that wasn't so important. But I vividly remember that my passion and love for salmon angling and for the river Namsen began that day. And it has never left me.

Upper Namsen near Fossland

179

After completing teacher-training college, I spent every free hour on the river, long summer holidays included. Arrangements with kind farmers allowed me access to the river – I got to fish and they got half my catch. No doubt who had the better deal!

My love of the Namsen has drawn me to its history. I am fascinated by the English gentlemen who pioneered salmon angling on the Namsen (and most other Norwegian salmon rivers). We called them "salmon lords", although I doubt many were actually members of the English nobility. One of the first of these was Mr. William Belton who visited the Namsen in 1837 and was so impressed with his experience that he wrote the classic, *Two Summers in Norway*. Another was Mr. Merthyr Guest who caught two fish totaling 100 pounds one day in 1894 and then paid what is reputed to be a small fortune to buy the cliff from which he caught the larger 64 pound fish. That promontory still bears his name, "Guest's Rock".

The heritage of these early English anglers can be seen in the flies, rods and reels we use today. Without their influence, we Norwegians would probably have continued for generations harvesting our salmon rivers for food alone, using only nets and other ugly tackle. We owe a great debt to them.

The Namsen with its mighty currents and strong salmon has seen me grow from a boy into a man, from chasing small brown trout to thrilling duels with silver torpedoes made of muscle. The salmon lords came to the Namsen to catch what they considered to be the ultimate challenge for the salmon angler – magnificent fish over 40 pounds. Are there any such fish left in the Namsen? Follow me down to the riverbank some day and you should find out!

Endre Aalberg

Hekton Beat

Upper Namsen near Fossland

ORKLA

IN THE OLD DAYS THE RIVER carried the shorter name Ork, which presumably comes from the Norse word "orka", which means work or labour. The steep canyon in the top part of "the working river" makes for challenging travel both for man and salmon, but as the river winds on further down a varied and vigorous cultural landscape catches the eye. The luxuriance of the Orkla valley has caused many fishers to lose their hearts to this beautiful river. Sitting down by the river bank, soaking in the rich nature and the company of good friends while the coffee is prepared over the open fire, is a strong part of the local fishing tradition. That's why resting benches or small fishing huts called "gapahuk" can be found by almost every pool.

The size of the Orkla is considered ideal by many fly fishers. It's big enough to house the fish of your life, but the width of the river will not leave you disheartened. It gives you the chance to cover most of the "hot spots" with a fly, but still produces more than enough challenges even for the experienced fly caster. With an abundance of beautiful fly water, and even a local Spey casting academy, it is not hard to see why the Orkla is often called "the fly fisher's river".

Templedogs or Sunray Shadows are often preferred in the beginning of the season, when the water is likely to be high. Later, when the water drops and its temperature rises, Thunder & Lightnings or Green Highlanders become good alternatives. Having said that, the man who arguably has had the most influence on modern Scandinavian salmon fishing, and who year after year finds his way back to the Orkla, Göran Andersson, says that in his experience profile and size are more important than pattern.

Many fishers have been amazed by the size, strength and stamina of the Orkla salmon. In June it is not uncommon to catch sea-liced fish as far up as 60-70 km from the sea, 250 meters above sea level. The early running salmon, many of them weighing 30-40 pounds, are eager to reach the wonderful spawning grounds in the upper parts of the river. These huge salmon want to be well positioned when the spawning starts in October, and with the increasing practice of catch-and-release among anglers, competition for reproduction gets fiercer by the year.

The Orkla enters the southernmost part of the Trondheim Fjord by the town of Orkanger. A travel along the Fjord will take you past the mouths of the

Vegard Heggem in Aunan Lodge Home Pool

Gaula, Nidelva, Stjørdal and Verdal, and 20 other smaller salmon rivers. The Trondheim Fjord is regarded by many as the world's most important fjord for Atlantic salmon. A large scale net buy out project in the Fjord, inspired and supported by Orri Vigfússon and the NASF, commenced in 2005. This will undoubtedly boost the unique stocks of multi-sea-winter fish for which salmon fishing in Norway has become so famous.

Vegard Heggem

David Goodman in Stasjonsholen Pool

Vegard Heggem in Strupen Pool

Page 185: Vegard Heggem in Oppstuggu Pool

STJØRDAL

THE STJØRDAL IS IN THE TOP echelon of Norwegian salmon rivers, usually one of the ten most productive each season. It is a large river with headwaters in Sweden that runs swiftly down a valley which provides major rail and road routes between the two countries. Salmon have access to some 50 km of the river from the Naustadfossen in Meraker to the small town of Stjørdal where it meets the Trondheim Fjord. Much of the river flows through classic Norwegian mountain scenery, and breathtaking pools of great charm and character perfect for fly fishing are strung throughout.

The river has been highly rated for its wonderful salmon fishing since it was first "discovered" by the early English angling pioneers in the mid-18th Century. Like the Alta and Gaula, it is closely associated with the history of salmon fishing in Norway. The first lease for a stretch of fishing on the Stjørdal was signed by Sir Henry Pottinger in 1858.

The Stjørdal is known for healthy runs of multi-sea-winter fish. In many pools there will be a specific lie which, year after year, is occupied by a very large fish – often exceeding the magical 40 pound mark. These leviathans can occasionally be seen jumping, and the splash can be so explosive it leaves no doubt that "Himself" is in residence. These huge fish are scarce and are usually quite capable of resisting the impulse to take your fly, but their mere presence stimulates the angler. Knowing the location of these lies, you can experience the indescribable thrill of drifting a fly over a possible fish of

Hembre Beat

a lifetime. If you do so during normal daylight, your chance of success is minimal. But it is a different matter beneath the mantle of the Norwegian "white night", especially at dusk or dawn. At these magical hours anything can happen. It is the time of hair raising, prickling expectation, combined with the still night air, the gleam of light in the sky, the darkened woods on the surrounding hillsides and the quiet murmur of the river's flow.

Another fond memory I carry from the Stjørdal is watching runs of fresh salmon coming in from the sea, which is not far away. We watch them head-and-tail as they come into the pool on their majestic run upstream. Sometimes they jump, like silver torpedoes, falling back with a loud splash. We know that at that moment they are not interested in our flies, but just watching them fills our hearts with joy!

Salmon runs on the Stjørdal have had their ups and downs. The river suffered the same fate as other grand Norwegian salmon rivers by having a hydro-electric dam built at its headwaters. And commercial netting has depleted stocks. The NASF-inspired plan to buy out the nets in the Trondheim Fjord resulted in an agreement that takes 80% of the nets out of production for five years beginning in 2005. Along with the other rivers that flow into the Fjord (including the Gaula, Orkla, and Nidelva), the Stjørdal enjoyed the first season of reduced netting last year. The net bag catch in the Fjord was reduced by 46 tons and the rod catch on these rivers went up by 27 tons compared to the previous year. The many more salmon that are now being allowed to return to their native rivers will strengthen spawning stocks and create new economic value for the community through an enhanced sport fishery.

Manfred Raguse

Farms along the River

EM

Em MEANS FOG IN THE OLD SWEDISH language and, if we look into the fog a little closer, we find a mysterious river shrouded in ancient oak trees, some over 600 years old. The river runs some 200 km from its headwaters in the middle of Sweden to its mouth on the Baltic. The water is dark with stones bigger than you can imagine, making wading a challenge. The kind of problem one can face is reflected in a passage written by Mr. Walter Barrett in his *A Fisherman's Memories & Methods*. Describing an incident that occurred while fishing with Gustaf Ulfsparre in 1929, Mr. Barrett writes: "Gustaf was watching me from the north bank. He shouted to me, "You can't go any further!" I thought he said, "You can go a yard further!" and relying on his intimate knowledge of his river, I stepped out and found myself swimming in deep water."

One cannot speak or write of the River Em without acknowledging the contributions of the immortal Gustaf Ulfsparre. He was the loving and devoted caretaker of the lower part of the river from the early 1900's until his death in 1987 at 93. During his tenure the river bed near the Baltic became so overgrown that salmon and sea trout had only a mile or so left in which to spawn. Gustaf cleaned the redds with machines and his bare hands, piece by piece, over a period of 17 years. It was hard and demanding work but he finally succeeded in saving the treasure of a river we have today. We must never forget him

Mill Pool

When the wind is right and you listen carefully while wading your way through a pool, you can sometimes hear a whisper from somewhere in the old oaks telling you to fish on and not be afraid. I remember one such whisper on a warm June evening telling me: "make a few casts more". So I did and, yes, your guess is right. A strong take came at the tail of the pool. Reflecting after a great fight, it suddenly dawned on me that the whispering voice I had heard was none other than the spirit of Gustaf Ulfsparre!

The history of this river is a paradox. Before the 1900's the river was full of strong salmon. In 1905 a power station dramatically cut the spawning area down to 30 km overnight. A few years later the next dam was built even closer to the Baltic Sea. With the salmon destroying themselves trying to jump the dams to reach their spawning redds, the sea trout saw their chance. Today the Em is a celebrated sea trout river, which still has a small (respectable) salmon run. Nowadays the salmon and sea trout can once again travel to some of their old spawning redds, and fishermen will land 600+ wild sea trout and salmon on average per year.

The Sea, Barrett or Nacken pools near the mouth of the Em are places to meet the sea eagle at dawn and tie on one of the old patterns created especially for this river – a Krafta, Supper Fly or Silver Dawn. When the old oaks are softly shimmering in green in the middle of May and the salmon enter, listen for the whispering voice: "Put on the Em Silver and make a few casts more …"

Pelle Klippinge

Home Pool

Göran Ulfsparre on way to river

192

Outflow to the Baltic Sea

MÖRRUM

THE RIVER MÖRRUM WAS FORMED around 8000 BC, carved by ice and run-off during the last glacial period. The ice withdrew from the Scandinavian Peninsula some 1000 years later creating a link between the Baltic Sea and the Atlantic Ocean. During the relatively short 500-year period the passage first was opened, Atlantic salmon entered the Baltic Sea. The link closed again and then reopened once more. But during the time the Baltic was a closed inland sea the salmon, which had migrated from the Atlantic, adapted to the Baltic and adopted it as their new winter feeding ground. This is why today we have two geographically and genetically separate groups of the same species – *Salmo salar*.

The ancient land records show that in the year 1231 the River Mörrum belonged to King Valdemar II. Thereafter, it was either the property of the King or the Church until it fell under State ownership, as it is today. Early in the last century English fly fishermen who came to explore the fishing potential of the Mörrum (as they did throughout Scandinavia) were convinced that the Mörrum salmon were impossible to catch on a fly rod. Fly fishing only took off in the early 1940's when the State opened the river for public fishing.

The River Mörrum is a "forest river" with large oaks, beeches and alder trees covering its banks and most of its drainage. Wading and Spey casting is indispensable. The river flows at a moderate pace, with slow, deep and generally short pools separated by runs of faster water. The water is tainted the colour of humus. The most beautiful time to fish the Mörrum is in early May when the river bank is a flood of white wood anemones contrasting with the fresh green leaves of beeches, and these signs of nature indicate that the first fresh salmon have entered the river.

The Mörrum is a nutritious river and provides a good start for its fast growing parr which are able to leave after just one year in the river. At their winter feeding grounds in the southern Baltic Sea the salmon feed exclusively on a rich diet of herring. The salmon return after two to four-sea-winters sturdy and strong and more than capable of justifying their species name, "the leaper". Almost every year salmon weighing over 44 pounds will be caught.

The early Englishmen were right – the Mörrum salmon will not easily rise to the fly. Days or sometimes even weeks can pass before you have any contact from a fish. But when you have finally duped one of these magnificent salmon, you will have an opponent who offers heavy and dramatic resistance.

Lars Terkildsen in Tjuva Hallen Pool

The wild salmon that survive today in the Mörrum have had to overcome the pollution of the Baltic Sea, hydroelectric power plants, commercial netting in their winter feeding grounds, netting in the river mouth, off-shore trolling by recreational fishermen and very intense fly fishing in the river. But the future is looking brighter. Paradoxically, the pollution that has contaminated the fish with such high levels of dioxin that they exceed EU's limit for human food might be the salvation of the wild Baltic salmon. Newly constructed fish paths now permit fish to bypass power plants to access their former spawning areas. Also, commercial fishing with drift nets will be banned in 2008. These developments will all help, but clearly the fly fishermen of Scandinavia must assume more responsibility in securing a long-lasting future for this beauty of silver.

Camilla and Jonas Hedlund

Footbridge

Pool 20

Jonas Hedlund under oaks

Page 197: Long cast, Camilla Hedlund

TANA

EUROPE'S MOST PRODUCTIVE salmon river, the Tana ("Teno" in Finnish) River, flows between Finnish Lapland and Norwegian Finnmark, acting as the border for 294 km. It begins as the Raja River in southern Finnmark, but the main Tana begins where the Inarijoki and Karasjoki meet. The river then flows 202 km to the Arctic Ocean, with the final 50 km entirely within Norway.

The Tana is rather shallow and features sandbanks and a generally flat river bed. The bottom is mostly sand and gravel, providing perfect spawning habitat, with rocks and boulders producing occasional rapids. With no lakes in the system, rain immediately affects the water level.

Salmon run all season long, but the height of the fishing season typically starts midsummer when the run is in full swing. In an average year some 30,000 fish are caught by commercial and sport fishermen, which represents about 15-20% of the entire European salmon catch. The record fish on the Tana weighed a staggering 80 pounds, but an "unofficial" 92 pound fish has been caught. The Tana has never been stocked and it serves as an enormous gene bank for Atlantic salmon.

English anglers arrived in the mid-19th Century, but fishing tourism did not really begin until the late 1950's when the highway to Utsjoki was completed. Today, the number of fishermen per year varies between 7,000 and 10,500. As each angler fishes an average of 3.5 days, some 30,000 day permits are sold each year -- this is serious fishing!

Tana boat

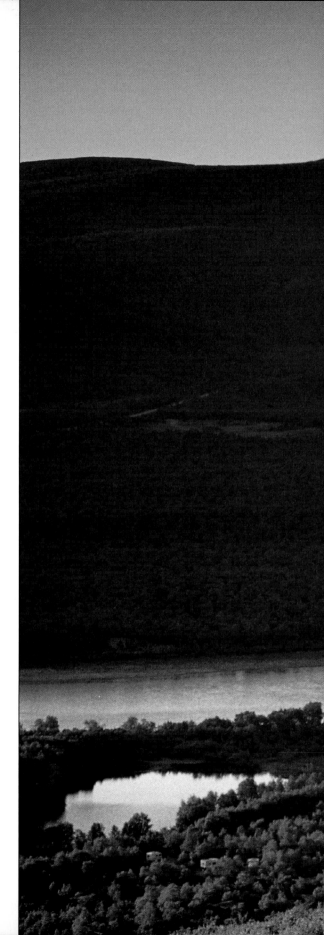

Fishermen in traditional Tana boat

The fishing is primarily focused on the Finnish side, where harling from a boat is the traditional method, especially in wider and shallower stretches. Fishing from the bank has become more and more popular, however, and fly fishing is increasingly common. The typical Tana fly was a 2/0-4/0 sparsely dressed classic salmon fly, but today's fly fisher utilizes the entire spectrum of flies, from drys to tubes. The most popular varies year to the year. The word goes out that a fisherman had a good catch with a particular fly (or lure), and anglers rush to buy it. Naturally, more and more fish are then caught with that fly. Suddenly it is everybody's favorite. The next year some other lure steals the show.

Fishing on the bank is concentrated in the narrower stretches of the river's middle run between Alaköngäs and Yläköngäs. The salmon run close to the bank and casts need not be long. The six km stretch of alternating rapids and runs at Alaköngäs attracts the most fishermen, and downstream at Särkät is also quite popular. Fishermen rotate through the best pools. Waiting in queue can take between a half to up to two hours, but new fish continuously running upstream give everyone a good chance. Those desiring more solitude and less waiting go upstream to the Karigasniemi area where the fishing is also good. Daytime provides the best fishing until early July, since the dirty snow melt tends to flow at night. By the second week of July the snow has usually melted, and the cooler water and low light of night is best. There is plenty of light at all hours! In late summer the fishing changes. Runs end and the salmon begin their search for spawning places. Should you spy one of these resident fish on the surface and make a decent cast, the thrill of a 50 pound fish splashing behind your fly will surely make your heart throb…

Markku Kemppainen

Near Utsjoki

FRANCE AND SPAIN

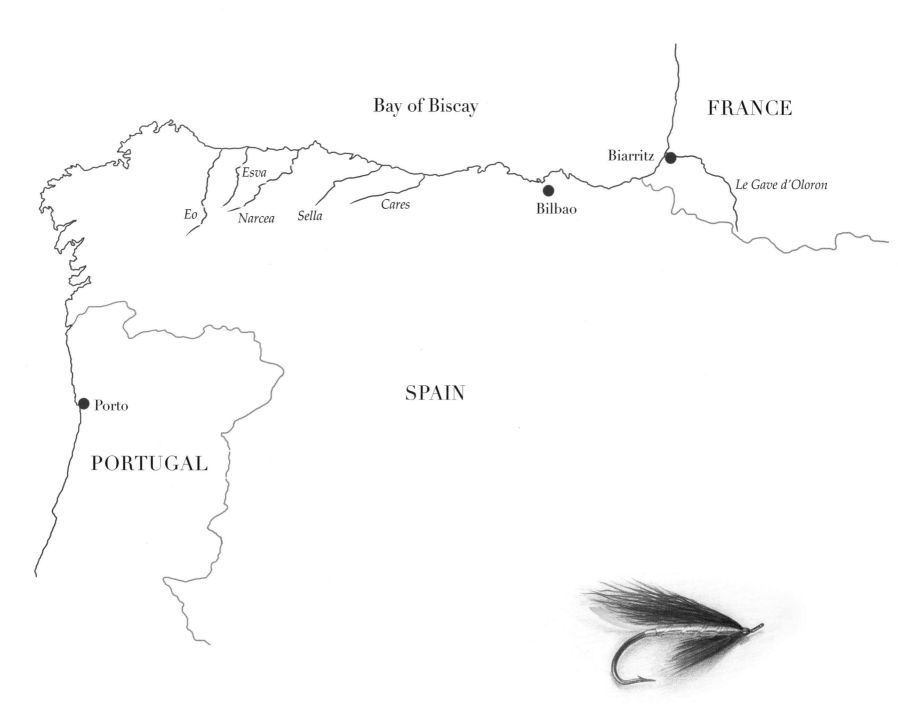

Bay of Biscay

FRANCE

Biarritz

Le Gave d'Oloron

Esva

Cares

Bilbao

Eo

Narcea *Sella*

SPAIN

Porto

PORTUGAL

13th century bridge over Gave d´Oloron at Sauveterre-de-Béarn

GAVE D'OLORON

Gave is the old gascon word for a watercourse that comes down from the Atlantic Pyrenees. The Gave d'Oloron, born in the confluence of the Aspe and Ossau at Oloron Saint Marie, joins the Gave de Pau 70 km downstream and throws itself into the Adour, the river that flows into the ocean at Anglet, near the resort city of Biarritz. The river is powerful, gushing from mountain snows and lowland rains, and pushes through landscapes rich with flora and fauna, and, of course, its emblematic fish: the Atlantic salmon.

In the Pyrenees, salmon was both the prince of fish and the fish of princes. Medieval lords and abbots collected tax payments in salmon and jealously guarded their commercial fishing rights. You can still see the traces today in the ancient deeds of the Abbey of Sorde, or the salmon-carved stone masonry of the Cathedral of Oloron-Sainte-Marie. For centuries salmon have been the prey of inventive fishing techniques and a source of human conflict. But it was the 20th Century that saw the worst destruction, most notably when dams were constructed that cut off access to much of the spawning area. By the 1930's salmon had totally disappeared from the Gave de Pau.

Flowing by town of Saucède

River view outside of Navarrenx

fishers and estuary netsmen worsened, a long history of wasted animosity that brought no help to the salmon. Only in the 1980's did a change in temperament appear – a desire to work together to save the salmon by regulating fishing and improving in-river conditions by building fish ladders. Besides personal efforts, important financial aid was granted by the public and private sector (and, of course, the NASF). Today the results are impressive, the spawning grounds have recovered and stocks at the start of this new millennium are showing a healthy progression.

Beautiful scenery, fast water, a wild but accessible landscape and salmon that can weigh over 20 pounds, plus mythical pools such as Masseys or the Bac d'Aren make the Gave d'Oloron France's premier salmon river. Sport fishing began here mainly thanks to the "English Circle in Pau", but was opened up to the general public by French laws that guarantee angling rights at low prices in public rivers. The river is broad and strong, and needs to be approached with care. Depending on the water height and season (from March to July), it can be fished with a range of techniques: spinners, natural bait or fly. Though there are certain regulations (such as fly-only periods), the overriding custom is one of courtesy amongst all fishers. There is even, perhaps surprisingly, a "World Salmon Fishing Competition", open to all comers, the prize being a picture in the local press and a couple of bottles of wine.

When I decided, 15 years ago, to fight for the restoration of salmon in our rivers, I promised not to fish again until the situation in the river was greatly improved, both for the fish and the fishers. Today I believe that the moment is not far away when I can take up my rod again and watch a silver flash engulf my fly.

Michel Maumus

Le Moulin de Susmiou dear Navarrenx

Typical Gave d`Oloron valley landscape

Page 207: Guide Hérve Baltar on Orin Pool

Cornellana Pool, Narcea

SALMON RIVERS OF ASTURIAS

Cares cutting through Picos de Europa

LOCATED HALF WAY ALONG the Cantabrian coast of northern Spain (*Mar Cantabrico* is the Spanish name for the Bay of Biscay), Asturias is the most bountiful salmon region in southern Europe. It is a coast of lovely beaches and colourful fishing villages with mountains rising to 2648 meters (8687 feet) close by. As well as endowing Asturias with breathtaking scenery, God saw fit to give it Atlantic salmon. Asturias has much to contribute to the betterment of mankind, including the salmon angler.

The Eo River is in the west of Asturias on its border with Galicia (which is directly above Portugal). A delightful river, it is not particularly large or deep, but it is ideal for early spring fishing. Its lush banks allow the salmon to rest in the shade, out of reach of anglers and free from the temptation of their flies. This river, which used to have plentiful large salmon, is currently undergoing a recovery following a major crisis which befell the salmon population in the 1970's. The Marquis of Marzales leased the river in the 1930's and was unstinting in his praise of it. March, April and May are the best times to catch salmon in this tranquil environment dotted with semi-derelict, slate-roofed hamlets.

Chanona Bridge, Esva

Pool on Narcea

209

Heading east, one next encounters the Esva, a beautiful but shallow river that currently produces few salmon, but with proper care could well become a popular spot for one-handed rod fishing. Then the Narcea, which until 1964 was the most majestic river in Spain for fly fishing. Its deep waters spring from high up on the mountains, home to bears and capercaillies (the largest member of the grouse family), and flow down through orange groves, all of which make it truly a natural wonder. Great golden boulders in the river provide natural resting places for the salmon that return year after year to this extraordinary part of Asturias.

The deep and mighty Sella River with its rapids and, in some stretches, white water descends to the sea from the province of Leon, at the foot of the Picos de Europa Mountains. It flows through the city of Cangas de Onis, Spain's first capital after the Arab Period, and ends in the town of Ribadesella in a long, gentle estuary. It is both beautiful and productive, being the number one river in Spain in terms of catches. It is also the most renown salmon river in Spain as much has been written about it. The Sella was General Franco's favourite river to fish, and during his rule the heavy poaching which had taken its toll on the Sella (as well as the other rivers of Asturia) during the Spanish Civil War was curtailed and salmon runs restored.

The Cares, the easternmost river in Asturias near its border with Cantabria, is appreciated by both anglers and non-anglers alike for its remarkably clear, crystal green waters. The clarity of its waters permits the riverbed to be seen for most of its length. Dramatic scenery unfolds before the angler where the river cuts through the huge limestone rocks of the Picos de Europa. Unpolluted and untouchable, it offers a perfect environment for salmon in its freezing water. The Cares could easily be one of Europe's greatest salmon rivers if it were given the care and attention it so richly deserves. It is also Spain's premier sea trout river.

Javier Loring Armada

Gin clear water of Cares

Early morning mist, Sella

Inviting stretch of the Eo

Page 211: Ancient bridge on the Sella

RUSSIA

Murmansk

Zolotaya

Rynda

Barents Sea

Kharlovka *East Litza*

Yokanga

THE KOLA PENINSULA

Ponoi

Rynda Camp

KHARLOVKA, RYNDA, EAST LITZA AND ZOLOTAYA

THESE FOUR RIVERS, all now part of the Atlantic Salmon Reserve, drain into the Barents Sea east of Murmansk on Russia's Kola Peninsula a couple of hundred miles north of the Arctic Circle, at the very limit of the Atlantic salmon range. This is wilderness fishing at the very edge.

The scenery is as old as Time, but it was only in the 1990's that the full potential of these unique rivers began to be realized, originally by a group of intrepid Swedes, and later by a man with a vision and a passion, Peter Power, who struggled through bureaucracy, costs and threats to establish the Atlantic Salmon Reserve, and preserve an enduring legacy to the salmon world.

Each river has its own character. Zolotaya, the smallest and most intimate, tumbling down a narrow valley; Rynda, bigger, but still requiring a careful approach and presentation; and then the two largest: Kharlovka, thundering down from the lake over three falls and slicing through grey rock in exciting canyon pools before opening out in the lower reaches into a classic broad valley; and finally the East Litza, the water carrying the faintest green tinge as it pushes between pinky-sandstone coloured cliffs, a short river that ends

Reindeer on Rynda

Home Pool, Zolotaya

Reindeer Crossing Pool, Rynda

abruptly for the salmon at its impressive waterfall. Resident and sea-run browns that would easily win any competition, and even a few humpback (Pacific) salmon, run in these rivers, but there is only one main event – *Salmo salar*. The records here are all in the mid and upper forties, and each spring a 50 pounder is hooked, but until 2006 no fisher had possessed the combination of stamina, luck and tackle needed to subdue one. Broken dreams and stories abound.

The season kicks off with the raw power of the ice out, sinking lines, the crunch of snow underfoot and brutal fishing for kelts and the ultimate in rock-hard silver. Fresh fish routinely strip off 200 meters of backing, leaving line burnt hands and worn out disc drags. It is a vain struggle to hold onto inexorable power. All may be lost, but revival comes with lunch on the river, huddled in a sheltered hollow, of hot soup, meat and salad, coffee and a candy bar and perhaps an afternoon nap. Then its out again to brave the icy water. Templedogs and heavy tubes search the deeps for pictures in gunmetal blue, pewter and white. It is indeed a long day that started hours ago crouched in the downdraft like a special forces team, watching the helicopter as it lifts and soars along the riverbank.

Summer comes quickly, with dwarf birch in leaf, flowers everywhere, the blues and purples of harebell and chives, and the less welcome buzz of mosquitoes. The wading is from hell - inching and probing with a wading

Kharlovka Home Pool

Waterfall Streams, Kharlovka

Looking down on Marks Pocket, Kharlovka

Kharlovka salmon

216

Peter Power in Peter´s Pocket, Zolotaya

stick around large boulders rounded to slippery perfection by millennia of current. Trembling hands cling on as hitched flies and bombers drag an enticing wake above huge fish, the adrenalin surges as a fish follows the fly, ending in an explosion of spray and hope…

Autumn follows with a carpet of scarlet berries, burnished golds and browns, the huge early-run fish now big old crocodiles, the rivers full of coloured salmon mixed with the sudden flash of deepest silver, the mysterious Osenka, an autumn run of remarkably fat, powerful salmon. Sea trout and arctic char come in on the tide, wood smoke wafts in the air, and Nature puts on its own display as the northern lights flicker across the polar darkness.

Gordon Sim

Snowbank Pool, East Litza

Releasing East Litza salmon

On the move, East Litza

Page 219: Paul Gragg in Tent Pool, East Litza

PONOI

No RIVER HAS GAINED SUCH an extraordinary reputation in just a few years. To the outsider, numbers of fish is what comes to mind when talking of the Ponoi and understandably so. In these modern times of salmon decline, a week where more than 1800 fish were landed in 2003 is a heartening event to any Atlantic salmon enthusiast. However, for those that have fished the Ponoi, their perception will be very different and for those that travel twice a year, in the spring and the autumn, the contrast of the seasons serves to generate yet another perspective. Spring not only brings abundance but the type of fishing that one could have only dreamt of. Fish, so free taking that some days it is almost ridiculous. They swirl, pounce and grab the fly with gusto and will often do so with such determination that it is not uncommon to witness the same fish time after time hitting the fly with its tail, bow waving and swirling until finally something in the fisherman's presentation induces a take.

The river is wide in spring but fines down quickly and can be fished from boat or bank. Both methods have their interests, centered on many miles of perfectly paced water with all sorts of structure forming micro-pools, which can be read as clearly as any small Icelandic river. It is clear where the fish will be with perhaps the most obvious being the mini-tails provided by large rocks or underwater structure that create tumbling draws over which one can skate a bomber. From the boat, the fun is to either fish to the high cliffs, which cannot be fished properly from the bank, landing the fly right next to the cliff and as the fly pulls away, so the take erupts; or to fish large tail-out glides with a long line and bomber skating proud like a yacht across

Ryabaga Camp tent

Middle Pumache Beat

221

a windless ocean. Here the salmon's bow-wave can start to show 10 yards behind the fly, following it for the duration of the swing, fisherman with heart in mouth.

Spring turns to summer and a whole new run of "summer run" fish arrive, from grilse to 20 pounders. The fishery becomes a more delicate environment, requiring small flies carefully presented, often with weeks dominated by the success of the skated muddler. Soon, the tundra beckons autumn and, some say, the most magnificent run of fish in the Atlantic salmon world. Big, broad-shouldered, silver brutes start to run and they want brash, colourful flies, which they hit with electrifying aggression. All these beautiful "fall run" fish keep coming as guests witness the explosion of autumnal colour on the tundra. They keep coming in their tens of thousands long after we anglers have gone south from this remote wilderness.

How did it get like this and how has it been sustained and become even better? The Ponoi was a lost secret until 1990, and it had benefited greatly from its very remote location and the fact that there are no roads. This "raw" resource was then nurtured by a joint effort between the Atlantic Salmon Federation and the Russian organisation PINRO lead by Dr. Sergei Prusov, including the removal of the net at the mouth of the river in 1994. These efforts lead to dramatic increases in parr and smolt densities, as well as the largest and longest running tag and release program in the Atlantic salmon world. Whatever one's taste in salmon fishing, the Ponoi is a fascinating place and a real beacon of hope for the Atlantic salmon fraternity.

Tarquin Millington-Drake

Guiding at Goldfish Bowl , Gold Beach

Page 223: Dusk over Ryabaga Home Pool

YOKANGA

THE YOKANGA IS THE THIRD largest river on the Kola Peninsula, flowing over 100 miles through the high arctic tundra of the Lovozero region and out into the Barents Sea. This is a rugged landscape of mirrored lakes and rolling hills covered in heathers and lichens, with grazing caribou, the occasional wolf, eagles, ptarmigan and many other species of birds and wildfowl to keep you company.

The Yokanga is quite unlike any other salmon river I have ever fished. It runs a rich dark tan colour, but beautifully clear, over a boulder-strewn river bed, meandering through an open landscape, swelling and slowing frequently into vast lakes, where the water warms in the Arctic sun, before gathering again and rushing headlong down short sections of sometimes fearsome rapids.

The Yokanga is no beginner's river. Just for starters, prepare to have your body clock well and truly shaken. Breakfast can be at 8 o'clock in the morning or 8 o'clock at night merely depending upon the weather. After breakfast a helicopter whisks you away up river – which is in itself a heck of a way to go fishing – dropping two of you, your guide and an inflatable dingy, in the middle of nowhere. You then fish down some four to eight km of river in a sort of shank's pony arrangement of walking and rafting in turns, before being airlifted back to camp.

Michael Barclay on Upper Nor Pool

Jeremy Herrmann in rapids below Lilyok Pool

225

You will also need to be able to overhead and sometimes spey cast at least 25 yards with a double handed rod into the necks and tails of the rapids and sometimes into the rapids themselves, but it is here that a riffled tube over a glassy glide can suddenly lift a huge snout followed by a broad black back, ending in a shovel-like tail that places your heart somewhere between your throat and your front teeth.

If the fish turns down the rapid, 200 yards of backing can evaporate in as long as it takes to write this sentence and a 30 pound leader might well seem like cotton. But if you are both lucky and skilful enough you might manage to coax your fish into the calmer waters of the lake where the fight could be slightly more evenly matched.

Should the battle end in your favour, the prize that lays at your feet is regularly a 20 pounder, more than occasionally a 30 pounder and perhaps even a 40 pounder.

Jeremy Herrmann landing fish in Nor Camp Pool

The Yokanga is now recognised as one of the greatest big fish salmon rivers in the world. PINRO (the Russian Polar Research Institute) scientists have classified the fish from the Yokanga as the largest genetic strain on the Kola and the records bare this out. In the 2002 season 46 fish of over 30 pounds were taken, two of which were over 40 pounds, the largest of which was estimated at just under 50 pounds. Not many rivers can make that kind of boast anymore.

For someone seeking the ultimate salmon fishing challenge in a true wilderness setting, the Yokanga is one of the world's finest destinations.

Michael Evans

Helicopter over Boulder Alley

RESTORING THE GREAT RIVERS OF YORE

The Skjern under reconstruction in 2001 with Lønborg Church in the foreground

THE RIVERS CELEBRATED IN THIS BOOK are among the finest Atlantic salmon rivers that remain more or less as nature intended. Sadly, they are only among the finest of the Atlantic salmon rivers that are left to us. Recent studies suggest that only about one third of the rivers where Atlantic salmon once ran now possess reasonably sustainable populations.

The Atlantic salmon has virtually disappeared from the rivers of Germany, France, Spain, Switzerland, Belgium, the Czech Republic and Slovenia and is tottering on the brink of extinction in the United States, parts of southeastern Canada and Portugal.

The plight of *Salmo salar* is, of course, not unique. Much of our wildlife has been destroyed or seriously depleted by practical necessity and man's insensitivity. Countless species of plants, animals and fish have now vanished from the earth. But there is something about the Atlantic salmon that motivates people to refuse to accept the prospect of its demise.

Fortunately for the salmon, its defenders are many and they are prepared to try mightily to reverse the decline of this marvelous fish and its rivers. Past traditions give them powerful help. The Atlantic salmon is deeply ingrained within the cultures of every country it has inhabited. The earliest known depiction of a fish is a sketch of an Atlantic salmon drawn in a cave in France 25,000 years ago. Salmon have been extolled in literature since man first developed the capacity to write, and carvings of salmon bedeck medieval cathedrals throughout Europe.

The salmon's role as an easily accessible, highly palatable and abundant food source was obviously a key part of its attraction. But the salmon's heroic attributes - its dogged determination to overcome predators, to navigate through boundless oceans to its native rivers and then to surmount mighty currents and falls over remarkable distances - further endears us to this incredible fish. Today the Atlantic salmon has a special place in the hearts of recreational fishermen. All who have tested their angling skills against *Salmo salar* understand why Izaak Walton dubbed it "the King of Fish".

Do read on because what follows highlights efforts to restore three rivers that were once amongst the world's finest Atlantic salmon rivers. They are chosen as inspiring examples of what can and is being done by committed conservationists (often led by a strong complement of devoted anglers) to restore the heritage of our beloved Atlantic salmon rivers.

Schaffhouse Falls in Switzerland

The Rhine near Zurzach and German border

THE RHINE

The Rhine is Western Europe's most important waterway. Rising in the alpine regions of Switzerland, it passes through Liechtenstein, Austria, Germany, Luxembourg and France before emptying into the North Sea in the Netherlands. It is 1320 km long, drains an area of 185,000 km2 and has countless tributaries, many major rivers in their own right, such as the Ruhr, Moselle and Alb.

The Rhine was historically a very productive Atlantic salmon river system. Salmon inhabited the river from its several mouths in the Dutch lowlands up to the famous Schaffhouse Falls in Switzerland, the natural barrier to migrating fish. Roman documents indicate how important salmon were as a food source from earliest times. A Swiss law still provides: "You must not serve salmon to your servants more than three times a week".

Salmon catches began their serious decline in the 19th Century with the construction of hydro dams and increasing discharges of industrial and domestic waste. The last salmon was caught in 1932. Remarkably, small runs of salmon briefly reappeared after WW II when dams below Basel were destroyed by bombs. But these were soon rebuilt, and the increased industrial activity and population explosion following the war resulted in industrial and domestic wastes pouring into the river untreated and unchecked. The Rhine Valley being one of the world's most heavily industrialized and populated areas, the Rhine became a flowing cesspool, toxic to fish and humans. The last wild salmon was caught in the 1950's.

The catalyst for taking action to clean up the Rhine was a release of toxic pesticides resulting from a catastrophic fire in a chemical plant above Basel in 1986. Much of the fish population of the river was destroyed and some species were wiped out entirely. The International Commission for the Protection of the Rhine (ICPR), a multinational organisation of all countries along the river, led the effort to address the pollution. Today water quality is constantly checked and industries that pollute the river are traced and heavily fined. Discharges of heavy metals, dioxins and pesticides have been substantially reduced. Nitrogen run off, primarily from agricultural activities, is still a problem, but the waters of the Rhine are once again comparatively clean.

But clean water is not enough. The multitude of dams, weirs, barrages and other obstacles which prevent salmon from migrating upstream to their native spawning areas must be addressed. This huge and costly undertaking is already well underway led by the ICPR and backed by strong public support. The construction of fish passes, modifications to sluices and other measures along the Lower and Middle Rhine have eliminated all insurmountable obstacles up to Iffezheim, some 700 km up river. But upstream from Iffezheim there are 10 barrages which still obstruct the 164 km of the Franco-German Upper Rhine to Basel. In 2000 a by-pass was constructed at Iffezheim which salmon have begun using in small numbers (390 were counted in 2004). Fish passages completed in April 2006 at Gambsheim have opened up the waters of the French river Ill and its tributary Bruche. Weirs have also been modified or equipped with fish passages in the Alb, Murg, Rench, Kinzig and Elz tributaries. But obstacles still remain in the Swiss High Rhine restricting access to the highly suitable spawning grounds located there. The tributaries Wiese, Birs and Ergolz still wait for the first salmon to spawn again in their waters.

The former stocks of wild Rhine salmon were not homogenous, but consisted of several distinct strains reflecting the differing conditions in the Rhine's many tributaries. All are now extinct, and salmon eggs must be imported for restocking purposes. The objective is to create new salmon stocks with a broad genetic variety offering more room for natural selection and adaptation to present habitats. During the past five years, some 11 million hatchery reared smolts have been released. In 2003, 2450 salmon were counted travelling upstream, and the actual number of migrating fish is though to be much higher. Studies indicate that a target of some of 7,000 to 21,000 returning adult salmon may be achievable in the not too distant future, with a self-sustaining population of wild salmon a possibility by 2020.

THE PENOBSCOT

When European settlers first arrived in the New World, rivers along the northeast coast of what would become the United States, from the Canadian border down to the Connecticut River, teemed with Atlantic salmon. Abundant salmon runs continued until the mid-19th Century when virtually every river with a significant flow was dammed to harness the power required by the Industrial Revolution. These dams, combined with commercial over-harvest, pollution and destructive land practices, had the predictable consequence - the prodigious salmon runs dwindled to a mere trickle. By the mid-1800's Atlantic salmon were extirpated south of Maine. Certain populations in Maine survived, but these too were severely depleted. In 2001, the Atlantic salmon was declared an "endangered species" and all fishing for salmon ceased.

Today, a landmark agreement on Maine's Penobscot River may well represent the last, best chance to restore Atlantic salmon in the US. The Penobscot is Maine's largest river system and one of the most ecologically significant rivers in the northeastern US. It drains roughly 9,000 square miles, or about one-third of the state, and historically held the state's largest populations of Atlantic salmon and other sea-run fish, with annual salmon runs estimated at 50,000-100,000 adults prior to 1830.

The river's lower dams are the single most significant remaining obstacle to the recovery of Atlantic salmon. 60 to 70 percent of all US salmon spawn in the Penobscot, but only three percent of the river's historic spawning habitat is below its lowermost dam. Today an average run of 1,000 salmon is supported by a federal hatchery which collects Penobscot specific brood stock each year as the salmon return from their feeding grounds off Greenland.

In June 2004, the Atlantic Salmon Federation, the State of Maine, the Penobscot Indian Nation, the federal government, dam owner PPL Corporation and several other conservation organizations signed an historic agreement to ensure the restoration of salmon and other migratory species while substantially preserving energy generation. Under the Agreement:
- A newly formed Trust has a five year option to purchase three dams for $25 million;
- The two dams closest to the ocean, Veazie and Great Works, will be removed;
- A state-of-the-art fish bypass will be constructed around a decommissioned third dam providing unencumbered fish passage;
- PPL Corporation will improve fish passage at dams further upstream;
- PPL Corporation has the opportunity to increase generation at several other facilities, resulting in the maintenance of most of their hydro power.

This project is desperately needed. Other attempts and tens of millions of dollars spent on efforts to restore salmon in the US have failed.

Penobscot River and Mt. Katahdin

The Penobscot Agreement addresses the root cause of the problem - high mortality associated with too many fish passages. It promises to be a cost-effective approach to restoring not only a self-sustaining run of 12,000 Atlantic salmon but other fisheries such as sturgeon, striped bass and herring. The Trust has embarked on an intensive campaign to raise the funds necessary to purchase the dams. Collaborative leadership made the agreement possible; likewise, collaborative funding from both public and private sources is critical to ensuring successful implementation of the deal.

Mouth of Skjern on Ringkøbing Fjord (before restoration)

THE SKJERN

In 1954 a tiny angler fishing on the River Skjern landed the biggest salmon ever caught by rod in Denmark. The fish weighed 26.5 kilos (58 pounds). The famous photo of the diminutive Mr. Dinesen with his gigantic catch is quite bizarre - he is obviously barely able to lift the fish and it covers up his body from toe to chin. This magnificent catch marked the beginning of the end for *Salmo salar* on the Skjern.

Back when the Danes dominated the North Sea region with their longboats, axes and adventuresome Viking spirit, the rivers of Jutland meandered slowly and pristinely through forested landscapes before emptying into the fertile feeding grounds of the North Sea. With perfect habitat, these rivers had prodigious runs of huge salmon. The River Skjern was the largest and most famous salmon river of them all.

The good old days for the Atlantic salmon in Denmark ended when the forests were cut down, the land was cleared and drained and the rivers were channelized, all for the sake of increased agricultural production. This process began in the mid-19th Century, and only accelerated after WW II. The Skjern and other Danish rivers were straightened out, levelled up and down and turned into canals serving no function other than the disposal of agricultural and industrial waste. Water tables fell, exposing layers of soil containing iron-sulphur compounds which drained into the rivers as sulphuric acid. By the 1980's all strains of Danish salmon were considered extinct.

Over the ensuing years desperate Danish anglers continued efforts to restock. A few fish would occasionally return, but efforts to substitute Irish and Swedish gene material were generally unsuccessful, both biologically and politically. Then in 1997 a miracle happened. Using scales preserved from before WWI, biologists were able to prove that a few of the salmon returning to the Skjern actually descended from the original strain. The chance to save the Skjern's unique strain of salmon, known for being fast growing and large, was a public and political sensation. The cry went up: "We must save the Skjern River salmon for posterity! And while we're at it, let's save the Skjern River itself!"

The Skjern restoration is the biggest and most expensive environmental project ever undertaken in Denmark. The bends in the river are being restored to slow the flow and permit natural flooding to re-occur (this effort actually began in 1989 to reduce excessive nutrient discharges into the North Sea which caused massive fish kills), spawning areas and other natural habitat is being restored and salmon are being restocked using the Skjern's unique strain. This year some 1000 multi-sea-winter fish returned to the Skjern and it is hoped that by 2010-12 the river will be largely self-sufficient. Recreational salmon angling is permitted, but on a highly restricted basis - one salmon per fisherman per year with no fishing at all permitted from 15 September to 16 April.

With the only surviving strain of native fish, no hydroelectric plants and a huge drainage area (one-tenth of Denmark), the Skjern is Denmark's best chance to restore a self-sustaining salmon population. If the restoration is successful, similar projects on Denmark's other salmon rivers will be reenergized. Denmark has many enthusiastic salmon anglers, all of whom eagerly await the day when they will no longer have to journey outside of their native country, like their Viking ancestors, to find salmon in abundance.

Max Gloor (Rhine)
Andy Goode (Penobscot)
Kurt Malmbak-Kjeldsen (Skjern)

LIST OF CONTRIBUTORS

Endre Aalberg was a career teacher until 1991 when he left the profession to devote himself to salmon fishing, its history and tourism, primarily related to his beloved Namsen River.

Øystein Aas is a professor of environmental sciences, a writer on salmon fly angling in Scandinavia and a director of NASF.

David Agnew is the chairman of one of the largest motor retailers in Northern Ireland and an Honorary Fellow of the Game Conservancy Trust.

Tony Andrews is the Chairman of the Scottish Countryside Alliance Educational Trust and has lived on the banks of the South Esk for most of his life. He is Chairman of its Angling Improvement Association.

Javier Loring Armada is a business man involved in international trade. He is a director of NASF and is a former president of *Real Asociacion Asturiana De Pesca Fluvial*, one of the oldest angling associations in Spain.

Archie Baillie is the Head Bailiff on the River Naver.

Einar Benediktsson is the managing director of the oldest oil company in Iceland and has fished his favorite river Grímsá for over 35 years.

Charles Bingham is the author of eight books on gamefishing and many articles. He lives in Dartmoor and has fished the River Dart for some 60 years.

Mark Brefka is an investment banker in New York City and a principal in an organization which acquires and preserves sporting properties for its membership.

Hoagy B. Carmichael is an authority on antique fishing tackle, and has both written extensively on, and long practiced the art of, making bamboo rods. He is the author of a recently published history of the Grand Cascapedia River.

Michael Charleston is a journalist who was appointed an Officer of the Order of the British Empire by Queen Elizabeth in 2005 for his salmon and wildlife conservation work. He serves as a strategic advisor to NASF.

Ian Cook is the Director of the River Exe Foundation and lives in a home overlooking the River Exe.

Duke of Abercorn is a company director, landowner and businessman who is deeply committed to rural conservation and preservation.

Gareth Edwards was one of rugby's most famous scum-halfs and played for Wales and the British Lions.

Uffe Ellemann-Jensen is the former Danish Minister of Foreign Affairs and the author of many books on international politics and one book on his favorite past time - salmon fishing.

Michael Evans is a professional fly fishing instructor with numerous angling videos, articles and tackle innovations to his credit. He lives and works near the small hamlet of Cowden on the Kent/Sussex border.

Padraic Fallon is a son of the famous Irish poet of the same name. He is chairman of an international financial publishing company based in London and is the author of a memoir published in 2003 .

Robert Gillespie has been a ghillie on the River Moy for 25 years. He is a certified instructor and guide, co-author of a book on salmon flies and winner of *Trout and Salmon Magazine's* "Conservationist of the Year Award".

Max Gloor is a banker who lives in Riehen/Basel, Switzerland, is an avid golfer as well as fisherman and is devoted to conservation activities, primarily those relating to fish.

Andrew Goode is an ecologist by training and the Vice President of the Atlantic Salmon Foundation in charge of U.S. Programs. He lives in Maine and is heavily involved in the Penobscot and other salmon restoration projects.

Max Hastings is a former editor of *The Daily Telegraph*, the author of some twenty books, three on country topics, and president of the Campaign to Protect Rural England.

Camilla and *Jonas Hedlund* live on the banks of the Mörrum River. He is a former Lieutenant Commander in the Royal Swedish Navy and is vice-chairman of the Mörrum Fishing Association. She is a teacher.

Vegard Heggem is a former Norway international footballer who played for Rosenborg B.K. in Norway and Liverpool F.C. in England. He now runs a fishing lodge at his childhood farm on the Orkla River and was actively involved in the Trondheim Fjord net buy out.

Sigurður Helgason is the former CEO and Chairman of Icelandair and is active in various conservation projects.

Jeremy Herrmann runs an international hedge fund in London and, among other accomplishments, won the individual world fly fishing championship in 1995.

David Hoare spends most of the week in Fleet Street in London where he has been Chairman of the oldest and last independent private bank in the UK and his weekends in Devon on his family estate.

Robert Jackson is a full time writer who lives in Iceland and the UK.

Bjarni Júlíusson is a computer scientist and chairman of the Reykjavik Angling Club, the largest association of sports fishermen in Iceland.

Markku Kemppainen is a publisher and dealer in fly fishing books, has co-authored three books and written numerous articles on fishing and conservation and was the founder of the Espoo Flyfishiers Club, the most active fly fishing club in Finland.

Kurt Malmbak Kjeldsen is the retired founder and CEO of an aquaculture company in Denmark who has written several books and articles on sea trout (which Denmark continues to have in abundance) and has served on the board of the Danish Salmon Fund, NASF's affiliated conservation organization in Denmark, since its founding.

Pelle Klippinge is a professional fly fishing instructor and guide who has written three books and numerous articles on fishing in Sweden. He is also a photographer and conservationist and lives on the banks of the River Em.

Steinar J. Lúðvíksson is an Icelandic author who has written more than 30 books, including one on the River Miðfjarðará. He has been editor in chief of a major magazine group in Iceland.

Michel Maumus is the Vice President of the *Conseil Générale des Pyrénées Atlantiques* and the *Institution Adour*, a French agency established in 1978 to manage and improve use of water resources in the Adour basin, including the restoration of migratory fish stocks.

Thomas McGuane is the author of thirteen books, many of which reflect his lifelong passion of fishing and the outdoors. He lives in Montana.

Tarquin Millington-Drake opened the London office of Frontiers International in 1993 and is one of its directors. He has been responsible for the operation of the Ponoi River Company since 1999.

Jóhannes Nordal is an economist by profession who served for many years as the Governor of the Central Bank of Iceland. He has also served as Chairman of the Board of the National Power Company and the Iceland Council of Science.

Donal C. O'Brien, Jr. is a lawyer by profession and a career conservationist. He has served as Chairman of the Atlantic Salmon Federation (U.S.), the National Audubon Society and the Connecticut Council on Environmental Quality and as Vice-Chairman of The Nature Conservancy.

Ragnar Önundarson is a retail banker. He formerly held executive positions with Industrial Bank of Iceland and Islandsbanki and is now the chief executive of Kreditkort hf. in Reykjavik.

Manfred Raguse has written numerous articles on salmon fishing and conservation. He was the founder of the Norwegian Flyfishers Club and is the proprietor of a hotel on the Gaula River for fly fishermen.

Len Rich is a former outfitter and a writer who has authored six books and numerous articles on the outdoors of Newfoundland and Labrador. He is also the originator of several salmon fly patterns.

Alastair Robertson is a freelance journalist who lives in Aberdeenshire and has fished the Deveron for 30 years. He writes a weekly shooting and fishing column for *The Scotsman*.

Alan Sanders and *Gordon Wigginton*. Alan lives on the banks of the River Dee in Wales and is past chairman of the Dee Fishing Association. Gordon is the proprietor of a hotel and health spa and, when not on the premises, can be found on one of his favorite pools on the Dee.

Þórarinn Sigþórsson is a private practising dentist in Reykjavík. He is the co-author of a book on the River Elliðaár and has written many articles and essays on salmon fishing.

Gordon Sim grew up in the Highlands of Scotland and has had a wide ranging and varied career. He is a senior police officer and is currently involved in various aspects of his favorite activity, salmon fishing. He serves as consultant to NASF and other organizations.

Michael Smith is a proprietor on the River Tay, a member of the Tay Board and a former Chairman of the Scottish Salmon and Trout Association.

Stewart Spence is the proprietor of a hotel on the banks of the River Dee and a tireless promoter of the river.

Bill Taylor is the President and CEO of the Atlantic Salmon Federation. He has written more than a hundred articles and essays on Atlantic salmon angling and conservation.

Andri Teitsson has held managing positions at several banks and investment companies in Iceland and is a landowner on three salmon rivers in Iceland.

Richard Vainer is in the diamond business, as a trader, consultant and valuer. He lives with his family on the Whiteadder, the first tributary of the Tweed, and fishes the Tweed over 70 days a year.

Orri Vigfússon is the founder and chairman of NASF.

Paul Volcker was Chairman of the Board of Governors of the Federal Reserve System of the United States from 1979 to 1987.

Olav Wendelbo is a river owner on the Lærdal and a former mayor of the Lærdal Commune.

Ken Whitaker is the former head of the Department of Finance of Ireland and a Governor of the Central Bank of Ireland. He is currently Chancellor of the National University of Ireland.

Michael Wigan is the manager of the River Helmsdale Salmon Fisheries Board in Sutherland, Scotland, and a writer on fisheries and fishing.

ACKNOWLEDGEMENTS

Many people in the Atlantic salmon fraternity participated in the production of this book and without compensation. It was a large group effort of almost exclusively volunteers. NASF is deeply grateful to its many friends and supporters who wrote the river descriptions. All are devoted salmon anglers and conservationists. They are listed above in the List of Contributors.

HRH the Prince of Wales, himself a salmon angler and deeply committed conservationist, did not hesitate to contribute the Foreword when asked.

R.Randolph Ashton, the young outdoor photographer who took most of the photographs over the summers of 2005 and 2006, was reimbursed for his expenses but otherwise received no compensation. His website is at **www.rrandolphphotography.com**

NASF would like to express its appreciation to these fine professional outdoor photographers who donated photographs for this book: *Michel Roggo* of Fribourg, Switzerland, **www.roggo. ch**; *Dale Spartas* of Bozeman, Montana, **www. spartasphoto.com**; *Matt Harris* of Cambridge, England, **www.mattharrisflyfishing.com** and *Palle Uhd Jepsen* of Swansea, Wales.

Thanks also to the following very talented photographers who contributed photographs: *Terry Ring, Vivvi Orrason, Tarquin Millington-Drake, Daniel Luther* and *Martin Neptune.*

The paintings of salmon flies were donated by a talented young Chilean artist, *Sebastian Letelier*, who specializes in painting fishing scenes, portraits and river maps and tying both classic and original salmon flies. His work can be seen on his website, **www. sebastianletelier.cl** and he can be reached at sebasletelier@yahoo.com.

Christine Twitchen is the artist that painted the beautiful map of the North Atlantic region appearing as the end papers in this book.

Many people gave guidance and other assistance, including *Roy Arris*, the publisher of the *Atlantic Salmon Atlas*, professional photographers *David Stoeklein*, *Charles Lindsay* and *Paul Nicklen* and the writers *Fen Montaigne* and *Chris Santella*. The Atlantic Salmon Federation was especially helpful with regard to the rivers of Canada and the Penobscot, and their President *Bill Taylor*, former U.S. Chairman *Donal C. O'Brien Jr.*, Vice President for U.S. Programs *Andrew Goode* and former New Brunswick Regional Director *Danny Bird* all willingly contributed their time and effort to help us.

We would also like to express NASF's gratitude to the many river associations and owners who allowed us access to their rivers to take the photographs. NASF was allowed access to certain of the rivers only as a special accommodation and because this book is primarily designed to promote conservation and restoration of our salmon rivers. We would also like to specifically thank all the many people who helped with the photographing, provided accommodations or otherwise assisted with the coverage of the rivers:

Alta: *Ivar Leinan*, Chairman of the Alta River Owners Association
Bann, Boyne and **Foyle**: the late *Newell McCreigh*, *Noel Carr*, *Robert Scott*, *Brian Hegarty* and *Robert Freeborn*
Blackwater: *Doug Lock* and *Michael Penruddock*
Dart: *Bill Robertson*
Deveron: *George Manson* and *Michael S.R. Bruce*, *The Rt. Hon. Lord Marnock*
Em: *Pelle Klippinge* and *Mortan A. Carlsen*
Exe: *Ian Cook*, Chairman of the Exe River Board
Gaula: *Manfred Raguse*, proprietor of the Storen Hotel on the Gaula

Gave d'Oloron: *Jacques Chouffot*, guide *Herve Baltar*, *Marc-Adrien Marcellier*, a director of NASF, *Michel Maumus*, Vice President, and *Francois-Xavier Cuende*, officer in charge of migratory fish, of the *Institution Adour*
Grand Cascapedia: *Marc Gauthier* and *Kenny Labrek* of the Grand Cascapdia Society and *Hoagy B. Carmichael*
Haffjarðará: *Anna* and *Einar Sigfússon*
Helmsdale: *Michael Wigan*, Manager of the Helmsdale Fisheries Board, and *Peter Quail*, Head Water Bailiff of the Helmsdale
Kharlovka, Rynda, East Litza and Zolotaya: *Peter Power*, Chairman of the Atlantic Salmon Reserve (which manages these rivers) and *Justin McCarthy*, Manager of the Kharlovka
Laxá in Leirársveit: *Gunnar Pedersen*
Lærdal: *Olav Wendelbo* and *Svend Brooks*
Miramichi: *Bill Taylor* and *Danny Bird* of the Atlanic Salmon Federation and *Mark Hambrook*, President of the Miramichi Salmon Association
Moise: *Donald Christ*, President, and *Yvon Letourneau*, Camp Manager, of the Moise Salmon Club
Mörrum: *Lars Terkildsen*, propriortor of the Mörrum flyshop
Moy: *Declan Cooke*
Namsen: *Tom Riise-Hansen*
Naver: *Archie Baillie*, Head Bailiff of the Naver
North and South Esks: *Tony Andrews*, Chairman of the Esk Angling Improvement Association
Orkla: *Vegard Heggem*, proprietor of the Aunan Lodge on the Gaula, and *David Goodman*
Ponoi: *Mollie Fitzgerald* of Frontiers International, and River Managers *Roderick Hall* and *Will Casella*
Restigouche: *Pete Dube*, proprietor of the Restigouche Motel, guide *Pierre D'Amours* and *Tom Tillingham*, Manager of the Restigouche Fishing Club

Rivers of Asturias: *Javier Loring Armada*, former president of *Real Asociación Asturiana De Pesca Fluvial*
Scottish Dee: *Stewart Spence*, proprietor of the Marcliffe Hotel, *Ellen Egan* and *Allan Sheppard*
Spey: *Iain Macdonald* and the River Spey Anglers Association
Stjørdal: *Jan Palmer Johennessen*
Tana: *Markku Kemppainen*
Tay: *Michael Smith*, a member of the Tay River Board
Þverá Kjarrá: *Gunnar Gíslason*
Tweed: *Richard Vainer*
Welsh Dee: *Alan Sanders*, Past Chairman of the Dee Fishing Association
Wye and Usk: *Stephen Marsh Smith*, Chairman of the Wye and Usk Foundation
Tyne: *Peter Gray*, a foremost authority on hatchery and stocking programs
Yokanga: *Justin Staal* of Frontiers International, River Manager *Mariusz Wroblewski* and *Michael Barclay*

NORTH

ATLANTIC

OCEAN